To the Shepherds

TO THE SHEPHERDS

A Call to the Watchmen

BY
Mitch Howell

RESOURCE *Publications* • Eugene, Oregon

TO THE SHEPHERDS
A Call to the Watchmen

Copyright © 2025 Mitch Howell. All rights reserved. Except for brief quotations in critical publications or reviews, no part of this book may be reproduced in any manner without prior written permission from the publisher. Write: Permissions, Wipf and Stock Publishers, 199 W. 8th Ave., Suite 3, Eugene, OR 97401.

Resource Publications
An Imprint of Wipf and Stock Publishers
199 W. 8th Ave., Suite 3
Eugene, OR 97401

www.wipfandstock.com

PAPERBACK ISBN: 979-8-3852-6700-2
HARDCOVER ISBN: 979-8-3852-6701-9
EBOOK ISBN: 979-8-3852-6702-6
VERSION NUMBER 12/24/25

Unless otherwise noted, all scriptures are from the KING JAMES VERSION, public domain.

"And that, knowing the time, that now it is high time to awake out of sleep: for now is our salvation nearer than when we believed."

—Romans 13:11 (KJV)

Contents

Author's Note | ix
INTRODUCTION: *A Cry from the Heart of God* | xi

CHAPTER 1: The Watchman's Warning | 1
CHAPTER 2: The Hireling Spirit | 5
CHAPTER 3: When the Platform Becomes a Throne | 9
CHAPTER 4: The Wolves Are in the Sanctuary | 13
CHAPTER 5: A Church Without Conviction | 18
CHAPTER 6: The Altar Is for Sacrifice, Not Entertainment | 23
CHAPTER 7: The Gospel of the Kingdom
   vs. the Gospel of Success | 26
CHAPTER 8: Repentance in the House of God | 31
CHAPTER 9: Ichabod and the Abandoned Altar | 37
CHAPTER 10: The Compromised Pulpit and
   the Silenced Prophets | 42
CHAPTER 11: The Great Falling Away Has Already Begun | 48
CHAPTER 12: Woe to the Shameless Shepherds | 53
CHAPTER 13: The Rise of the Remnant Watchmen | 59
CHAPTER 14: Merchandising the Anointing | 64
CHAPTER 15: The Hirelings Who Scattered My Sheep | 70
CHAPTER 16: A Church Without Conviction | 75
CHAPTER 17: The Gospel That Costs Nothing,
   Changes Nothing | 80
CHAPTER 18: A Call to the New Shepherds | 85

CONTENTS

CHAPTER 19: Entertained but Not Transformed | 91
CHAPTER 20: A Church Without Conviction | 96
CHAPTER 21: Shepherds, Wake the Sleeping Flock | 100
CHAPTER 22: When the Pulpit Lost Its Tears | 105
CHAPTER 23: Scattered by Silence, Wounded by Words | 110
CHAPTER 24: The Weight and Wonder of the Call | 115
CHAPTER 25: Strength for the Weary Shepherd | 122
CHAPTER 26: Guarding the Flock in the Last Days | 127
CHAPTER 27: Leading the Sheep Back to the Altar | 132
CHAPTER 28: Feeding the Sheep, Not Entertaining the Goats | 136
CHAPTER 29: The Chief Shepherd Is Coming | 140
CHAPTER 30: A Call to the Watchmen | 146

Final Word | 152
About the Author | 153

Author's Note

This book is not written to win applause, but to sound an alarm. I know the words within these pages may offend. They may stir anger. Some may reject them outright. But the truth of God's word has never been popular, and it is not mine to soften.

I do not write as one who is perfect. I am a man who has stumbled, sinned, and been broken. But I am also a man who has been forgiven, washed in the blood of Jesus Christ, and called to obedience. Out of that place, I can only say what the Lord has placed in my spirit.

If these words wound, may they be the wounds of a friend; wounds that cut only so healing can come. My heart is not to condemn, but to call. Not to tear down, but to awaken.

The days are short. The hour is late. And I would rather be hated for speaking truth than loved for staying silent. If one soul repents, if one shepherd returns to the altar, if one church recovers the fear of the Lord, then every word and every reproach will be worth it.

To God alone be the glory.

INTRODUCTION: **A Cry from the Heart of God**

To the Shepherds: A Call to the Watchmen is a trumpet blast in a weary generation—a plea from the heart of the Father to His shepherds and servants who have wandered from their posts. These pages carry a call to return, not to religion, but to righteousness, not to programs, but to His presence.

This message is not born of judgment, but of love—a love that warns, corrects, and restores. It speaks to pulpits that have grown dim, to watchmen whose eyes have closed, and to leaders who once stood in awe of His glory but have settled for comfort.

Rooted firmly in Scripture, this cry calls the church back to the foundations that were never meant to change: holiness, repentance, and the fear of the Lord. It is a reminder that the God who once thundered on Sinai still whispers to those who will listen in the secret place.

If conviction comes as these words are read, let it be seen as mercy—for God still calls His shepherds by name. The trumpet is sounding. The night is far spent. It is time to return to the altar, for the hour is late and the harvest is waiting.

CHAPTER 1: The Watchman's Warning

EZEKIEL 33:7–9 (KJV)

"So thou, O son of man, I have set thee a watchman unto the house of Israel; therefore thou shalt hear the word at my mouth, and warn them from me.

When I say unto the wicked, O wicked man, thou shalt surely die; if thou dost not speak to warn the wicked from his way, that wicked man shall die in his iniquity; but his blood will I require at thine hand.

Nevertheless, if thou warn the wicked of his way to turn from it; if he do not turn from his way, he shall die in his iniquity; but thou hast delivered thy soul."

The Lord is raising up watchmen in this hour, but many who were called to stand on the wall have abandoned their posts. The trumpet has fallen silent in the very generation that needs it most. Shepherds have traded the fire of the altar for the applause of men. The urgency of eternity has been exchanged for the comfort of the present. And the sheep are wandering—unguarded, unled, and unprepared.

A watchman does not exist to be liked. A watchman exists to warn. And the word of God is clear: if we fail to sound the alarm, the blood of the people will be required at our hands. This is not an optional duty. It is a holy assignment. A shepherd who refuses to warn the sheep has ceased to be a shepherd and has become a hireling.

> ISAIAH 56:10–11 (KJV)
>
> *"His watchmen are blind: they are all ignorant, they are all dumb dogs, they cannot bark; sleeping, lying down, loving to slumber.*
>
> *Yea, they are greedy dogs which can never have enough, and they are shepherds that cannot understand: they all look to their own way, every one for his gain, from his quarter."*

This is the tragedy of our time. Men who once trembled at the word now tremble at the thought of losing members. Pastors who once thundered "Thus saith the Lord" now murmur motivational clichés. Altars that once burned with repentance now collect dust. And yet the wolves are circling. The enemy has not gone silent; then why has the church?

The calling of a shepherd is not to entertain, but to intercede. Not to soothe, but to sound the alarm. Not to feed self, but to feed the flock of God. A watchman who will not warn is worse than no watchman at all, for he gives the illusion of safety while danger approaches.

> JEREMIAH 6:17 (KJV)
>
> *"Also I set watchmen over you, saying, Hearken to the sound of the trumpet. But they said, We will not hearken."*

This is the rebellion of our day. God is still speaking. His watchmen are still sounding the trumpet. But multitudes cover their ears, preferring entertainment to exhortation, preferring comfort to conviction. Yet the command remains: warn them, whether they will hear or whether they will forbear.

CHAPTER 1: THE WATCHMAN'S WARNING

This book is not written for applause. It is written as a trumpet blast. A call to repentance. A cry to shepherds, pastors, and leaders who still have ears to hear. The blood of souls is too high a price to pay for silence.

TRUMPET CALL

- Rise up, watchmen of God! Take your place on the wall.
- Do not remain silent while wolves devour the flock.
- Refuse compromise. Sound the trumpet. Preach the cross. Warn with tears.
- The blood of this generation must not be found on your hands.

DECLARATION

I will not be silent when God calls me to speak.

I will not seek comfort when the flock is in danger.

I will stand as a watchman on the wall, faithful to the word, obedient to the Spirit, and unashamed of the gospel.

By His grace, I will sound the trumpet until my final breath.

CHAPTER 2: The Hireling Spirit

JOHN 10:12–13 (KJV)

"But he that is an hireling, and not the shepherd, whose own the sheep are not, seeth the wolf coming, and leaveth the sheep, and fleeth: and the wolf catcheth them, and scattereth the sheep.

The hireling fleeth, because he is an hireling, and careth not for the sheep."

The greatest danger to the church has never been the wolf at the gate, but the hireling in the pulpit. Wolves are easy to identify; they openly hate the truth, mock the word, and devour the sheep. But hirelings are more dangerous because they pretend to be shepherds while lacking the heart of the Chief Shepherd.

A hireling may look polished, speak well, and fill a building, but when the wolf comes—when the culture presses in, when the truth costs something, when persecution arises—the hireling runs. Why? Because the sheep were never his burden, only his platform.

The tragedy of our time is that pulpits across the land are filled with hirelings. They love the microphone more than the mandate. They love the applause more than the altar. They love the perks of ministry, but not the pain of intercession.

TO THE SHEPHERDS

Ezekiel 34:2–4 (KJV)

"Son of man, prophesy against the shepherds of Israel, prophesy, and say unto them, Thus saith the Lord GOD unto the shepherds; Woe be to the shepherds of Israel that do feed themselves! should not the shepherds feed the flocks?

Ye eat the fat, and ye clothe you with the wool, ye kill them that are fed: but ye feed not the flock.

The diseased have ye not strengthened, neither have ye healed that which was sick, neither have ye bound up that which was broken, neither have ye brought again that which was driven away, neither have ye sought that which was lost; but with force and with cruelty have ye ruled them."

This is the hireling spirit: feeding self instead of the sheep. It is a betrayal of the call. It is the heart of Cain, who said, "Am I my brother's keeper?" It is the spirit of Judas, who kissed Jesus but sold Him for silver. It is the sin of Eli's sons, who despised the altar while fattening themselves on what belonged to God.

The hireling spirit is alive today. It dresses in designer suits, stands under bright lights, and preaches sermons that never offend. It knows how to brand, how to market, how to grow a following, but not how to weep between the porch and the altar. It builds churches without building disciples. It multiplies services but never multiplies holiness.

Jeremiah 23:1–2 (KJV)

"Woe be unto the pastors that destroy and scatter the sheep of my pasture! saith the LORD.

Therefore thus saith the LORD God of Israel against the pastors that feed my people; Ye have scattered my flock, and driven them away, and have not visited them: behold, I will visit upon you the evil of your doings, saith the LORD."

CHAPTER 2: THE HIRELING SPIRIT

Woe. Not warning. Not suggestions. Woe. God Himself promises judgment on shepherds who abandon their post. This is not about church growth, but about eternal souls. Every soul neglected, every sin excused, every warning silenced; God sees, and God will judge.

The hireling spirit avoids the message of the cross because it offends. It avoids the call to holiness because it convicts. It avoids preaching on sin because it might empty the pews. And in doing so, it betrays Christ Himself, who came not to entertain but to transform.

But a true shepherd lays down his life for the sheep. He warns, even if they will not listen. He preaches holiness, even if the offerings shrink. He weeps over sin, even if the world mocks. A true shepherd is not measured by numbers but by faithfulness.

ACTS 20:26–27 (KJV)

"Wherefore I take you to record this day, that I am pure from the blood of all men.

For I have not shunned to declare unto you all the counsel of God."

Paul was not a hireling. He preached the full counsel of God—sin, repentance, judgment, grace, and holiness. He did not withhold the truth to keep a crowd. He did not tailor the gospel to fit culture. He stood as a faithful shepherd, and he was willing to bleed for it.

Shepherds of today, the call is clear: reject the hireling spirit. Lay down your life for the sheep. Preach the word in season and out of season. Refuse the temptation to entertain. Guard the flock entrusted to you, even if it costs everything.

TRUMPET CALL

- Woe to the hirelings who feed themselves and neglect the sheep!
- Rise up, shepherds of God, and take your place on the wall.
- Preach the cross, preach repentance, preach holiness—no matter the cost.
- The Lord is inspecting His house, and He will separate the true from the false.

DECLARATION

I renounce the spirit of the hireling.

I will not feed myself while the sheep starve.

I will preach the word in fullness, without fear of man.

I will stand faithful to Christ, the Chief Shepherd, and to the flock entrusted to me.

When the wolves come, I will not run; I will stand in His strength and guard His sheep.

CHAPTER 3: When the Platform Becomes a Throne

Isaiah 42:8 (KJV)

"I am the LORD: that is my name: and my glory will I not give to another, neither my praise to graven images."

The pulpit was never meant to be a stage. The altar was never meant to be a platform for men. Yet in our generation, many shepherds have turned the holy desk into a throne, a place not of trembling obedience, but of performance, pride, and self-exaltation.

We were called to preach Christ crucified, but too many now preach themselves. The messenger has become the message. Sermons are no longer birthed in prayer closets, but in boardrooms and marketing sessions. The focus has shifted from souls to seats, from holiness to hype, from feeding the sheep to feeding egos.

2 Corinthians 4:5 (KJV)

"For we preach not ourselves, but Christ Jesus the Lord; and ourselves your servants for Jesus' sake."

When the platform becomes a throne, ministry becomes about reputation, not repentance. Leaders are treated like celebrities instead of servants. Applause replaces the anointing. Followers replace fruit. And the church begins to mirror the world more than her Savior.

This is not new. King Saul fell into the same trap, loving the sound of his own name more than the honor of God. When confronted by Samuel, Saul confessed, "I have sinned: yet honour me now, I pray thee, before the elders of my people" (1 Sam 15:30). His concern was not for God's glory, but for his own image. And God rejected him as king.

How many today are walking the same path? Shepherds who once trembled at the word now tremble at the thought of losing followers. Men who once wept at the altar now perform at the platform. Leaders who once cried, "Not unto us, O Lord," now secretly whisper, "Look at me."

Matthew 23:12 (KJV)

"And whosoever shall exalt himself shall be abased; and he that shall humble himself shall be exalted."

The throne belongs to Christ alone. To exalt self in His house is idolatry. To use His platform for personal glory is theft of the highest order, stealing glory from the One who will not share it.

And the cost is deadly. Pride precedes destruction. When the platform becomes a throne, the anointing departs. When the pulpit is polluted by ego, the glory lifts. When the shepherd is more visible than the Savior, the sheep are led not to Christ, but to ruin.

Jeremiah 9:23-24 (KJV)

"Thus saith the LORD, Let not the wise man glory in his wisdom, neither let the mighty man glory in his might, let not the rich man glory in his riches:

But let him that glorieth glory in this, that he understandeth and knoweth me, that I am the LORD which exercise lovingkindness, judgment, and righteousness, in the earth: for in these things I delight, saith the LORD."

CHAPTER 3: WHEN THE PLATFORM BECOMES A THRONE

We must return to trembling. To pulpits that quake under the weight of God's presence. To sermons birthed in tears, not tailored for applause. To shepherds who point relentlessly to Jesus, refusing to be seen themselves. The platform must once again become an altar, not a throne.

Shepherds, this is not about your brand, your following, or your success. It is about eternity. It is about the blood of souls. It is about the glory of Christ, who alone is worthy. Cast down your crowns. Step off your thrones. Return to the place of brokenness before God.

TRUMPET CALL

- The platform is not your throne; it belongs to Christ alone.
- Reject celebrity Christianity. Return to servanthood.
- Preach Christ crucified, not yourself exalted.
- The pulpit is holy ground; tremble again before you step upon it.

DECLARATION

I will not exalt myself above the flock or the cross.

I will not turn the pulpit into a platform for pride.

I will humble myself before the Lord, that His glory may be revealed.

I will preach not myself, but Christ Jesus as Lord, and myself only as His servant.

The platform is not my throne; it is His altar.

CHAPTER 4: The Wolves Are in the Sanctuary

ACTS 20:29–30 (KJV)

"For I know this, that after my departing shall grievous wolves enter in among you, not sparing the flock.

Also of your own selves shall men arise, speaking perverse things, to draw away disciples after them."

Paul's warning has come to pass. Wolves have not only crept into the flock; they now stand in pulpits. They no longer prowl at the edges; they preach in the sanctuaries. They wear the right clothes, carry the right Bible, and use the right phrases. But their hearts are corrupt, and their motives are deadly. And what is worse: many shepherds have stayed silent while the sheep are devoured.

Wolves do not walk in snarling and obvious. They enter in sheep's clothing. They smile, they flatter, they promise peace. But underneath, they are ravenous. They twist the word to suit their agendas. They prophesy lies to gain followers. They feed themselves while the flock starves.

MATTHEW 7:15–16 (KJV)

"Beware of false prophets, which come to you in sheep's clothing, but inwardly they are ravening wolves.

Ye shall know them by their fruits. Do men gather grapes of thorns, or figs of thistles?"

The fruit tells the truth. Wolves cannot produce holiness. They cannot produce repentance. They cannot produce obedience. They may fill buildings, but they empty heaven. Their followers clap and shout, but they are still bound by sin. This is the deception of our hour; the crowd mistakes hype for holiness.

2 Peter 2:1–3 (KJV)

"But there were false prophets also among the people, even as there shall be false teachers among you, who privily shall bring in damnable heresies, even denying the Lord that bought them, and bring upon themselves swift destruction.

And many shall follow their pernicious ways; by reason of whom the way of truth shall be evil spoken of.

And through covetousness shall they with feigned words make merchandise of you: whose judgment now of a long time lingereth not, and their damnation slumbereth not."

Wolves always turn God's people into merchandise. The offering plate is their god. The stage lights are their altar. They preach not because they fear God but because they crave gain. They do not tremble before the word; they twist it for profit. And many follow them. Why? Because the flesh loves a false gospel.

Jude 4 (KJV)

"For there are certain men crept in unawares, who were before of old ordained to this condemnation, ungodly men, turning the grace of our God into lasciviousness, and denying the only Lord God, and our Lord Jesus Christ."

CHAPTER 4: THE WOLVES ARE IN THE SANCTUARY

Grace is now twisted into license. Wolves tell the sheep, "God understands your sin. Don't feel condemned. Live as you want; grace covers it all." But the word says the opposite: "Shall we continue in sin, that grace may abound? God forbid" (Rom 6:1-2). Wolves strip the cross of its call to holiness. They offer heaven without repentance, blessings without obedience, Christ without the cross.

And pulpits remain silent. Shepherds excuse themselves: "It's not my place to judge." But silence is complicity. To refuse to warn is to share in the guilt.

> EZEKIEL 33:6 (KJV)
>
> *"But if the watchman see the sword come, and blow not the trumpet, and the people be not warned; if the sword come, and take any person from among them, he is taken away in his iniquity; but his blood will I require at the watchman's hand."*

Shepherd, the blood of this generation is at stake. If you refuse to blow the trumpet, their blood is on your hands. If you allow wolves to preach unchecked, their blood is on your hands. If you stand by while deception spreads, their blood is on your hands.

This is not about being "divisive." This is about being faithful. Better to be hated by men than to be guilty before God.

> JEREMIAH 23:16 (KJV)
>
> *"Thus saith the LORD of hosts, Hearken not unto the words of the prophets that prophesy unto you: they make you vain: they speak a vision of their own heart, and not out of the mouth of the LORD."*

Wolves speak visions of their own heart. They prophesy out of imagination, not revelation. They speak dreams that flatter but never convict. But the word of God is a fire and a hammer (Jer 23:29). If the sermon does not burn and break, it is not of God.

God is raising up shepherds who will no longer tolerate wolves. Who will call them out by name if needed. Who will guard the sheep even at the cost of popularity. This is the moment for courage. This is the hour for boldness. This is the season for watchmen to take their place on the wall again.

CHAPTER 4: THE WOLVES ARE IN THE SANCTUARY

TRUMPET CALL

- Wolves are no longer outside the gate; they are in the sanctuary.
- Shepherds, awaken! Blow the trumpet, drive them out, guard the flock.
- Call deception what it is. Preach holiness, preach the blood, preach repentance.
- The silence of shepherds is as deadly as the lies of wolves.

REFLECTION QUESTIONS

1. Have I been silent about wolves because of fear of man?
2. Do I measure sermons by applause or by repentance?
3. Am I more afraid of offending people than of offending God?
4. Would God call me faithful if He inspected how I guarded His flock today?

DECLARATION

I will not be silent while wolves devour the flock.

I will not tolerate false gospels or false shepherds.

I will guard the sheep entrusted to me with the word of God.

I will preach holiness, repentance, and the cross without compromise.

By His Spirit, I will be a faithful watchman until Christ returns.

CHAPTER 5: **A Church Without Conviction**

2 Timothy 3:5 (KJV)

"Having a form of godliness, but denying the power thereof: from such turn away."

We are living in an age of appearances. Churches are full, music is loud, branding is polished, and sermons are clever, but much of it is powerless. What Paul saw in his day, we are drowning in now: a form of godliness, but denying the power thereof.

The church has become skilled at looking alive while being dead. We know how to stir emotions, but not how to pierce hearts. We know how to organize events, but not how to call men to repentance. We have filled our sanctuaries with sound, but the sound of weeping at the altar is gone.

A church without conviction is not the church of Jesus Christ; it is a shell, a stage play, a religious illusion.

Jeremiah 6:14 (KJV)

"They have healed also the hurt of the daughter of my people slightly, saying, Peace, peace; when there is no peace."

This is the message of pulpits without fire: "Peace, peace." They tell sinners that God is fine with their compromise. They assure the

CHAPTER 5: A CHURCH WITHOUT CONVICTION

rebellious that grace requires no repentance. They hand out comfort when people need correction. They tell men they are whole when they are dying.

This is the deadliest kind of deception: healing wounds slightly. A powerless church leaves the cancer of sin untouched.

HEBREWS 4:12 (KJV)

"For the word of God is quick, and powerful, and sharper than any twoedged sword, piercing even to the dividing asunder of soul and spirit, and of the joints and marrow, and is a discerner of the thoughts and intents of the heart."

The word of God is supposed to pierce, cut, and divide. Conviction is not cruelty; it is mercy. The scalpel hurts, but it heals. Conviction burns, but it purifies. Conviction breaks, but it rebuilds.

Where there is no conviction, there can be no repentance. And without repentance, there is no salvation. This is why Satan loves pulpits without fire; they may gather crowds, but they do not rescue souls.

REVELATION 3:15–16 (KJV)

"I know thy works, that thou art neither cold nor hot: I would thou wert cold or hot.

So then because thou art lukewarm, and neither cold nor hot, I will spue thee out of my mouth."

This is Christ's response to a powerless church: disgust. He does not say, "At least you tried." He says, "I will spue thee out of my mouth." The lukewarm church nauseates Christ.

A church without conviction sings but does not repent, claps but does not obey, gathers but does not surrender. And Christ Himself will reject it unless it repents.

ISAIAH 66:2 (KJV)

"But to this man will I look, even to him that is poor and of a contrite spirit, and trembleth at my word."

God is not looking for polished programs; He is looking for trembling hearts. A church that does not tremble at the word is a church that has lost its first love.

Holiness is not optional. Repentance is not outdated. Brokenness is not weakness. These are the very marks of the true church. When they are absent, what remains is a powerless institution, not the bride of Christ.

AMOS 8:11-12 (KJV)

"Behold, the days come, saith the Lord GOD, that I will send a famine in the land, not a famine of bread, nor a thirst for water, but of hearing the words of the LORD:

And they shall wander from sea to sea, and from the north even to the east, they shall run to and fro to seek the word of the LORD, and shall not find it."

We are already in this famine. Churches gather weekly, yet the word of the Lord is rare. People run from conference to conference, desperate for a word, but leave unfed because pulpits refuse to thunder with repentance.

The famine is not because the Bible is absent; it is because conviction is silenced.

PSALM 85:6 (KJV)

"Wilt thou not revive us again: that thy people may rejoice in thee?"

CHAPTER 5: A CHURCH WITHOUT CONVICTION

Revival does not come through entertainment or programs. It comes when conviction returns. It comes when the church falls on its face and cries out for mercy. It comes when the word of God pierces again and sinners cry out, "What must I do to be saved?"

Until the pulpits tremble again, the people will not. Until the preachers weep again, the altars will not be filled.

TRUMPET CALL

- A church without conviction is a church without Christ.
- Stop soothing sinners; call them to repentance.
- Without conviction, there is no repentance. Without repentance, there is no salvation.
- Shepherds, weep between the porch and the altar again. Let the altars burn.

REFLECTION QUESTIONS

1. Do I preach sermons that pierce hearts or ones that protect comfort?
2. When was the last time conviction broke me before the Lord?
3. Am I producing disciples or entertaining members?
4. Do I measure fruit by applause or by repentance?
5. Would Christ call my church hot, cold, or lukewarm?
6. Have I silenced conviction to gain the approval of men?

DECLARATION

I refuse to preach a powerless gospel.

I will not silence conviction to protect myself.

I will declare the word of God in its fullness—sin, holiness, repentance, judgment, and the cross.

I will live trembling before the Lord so His presence is never absent from my life.

I will measure ministry not by numbers, but by fruit—lives transformed by conviction.

By His Spirit, I will be a voice of fire in a generation gone cold.

CHAPTER 6: The Altar Is for Sacrifice, Not Entertainment

LEVITICUS 6:13 (KJV)

"The fire shall ever be burning upon the altar; it shall never go out."

The altar was never meant to be a stage. In the Old Testament, the altar was a place of death, where something had to die before God. It was a place of sacrifice, surrender, and holy fire. The fire on the altar was commanded by God to never go out, because the altar was not for men's amusement but for God's glory.

But in our generation, the altar has been turned into a stage. The fire has been replaced by fog machines. The cries of repentance have been replaced by applause. Where once men trembled and wept, now they clap and cheer. Where once the fire of God consumed sin, now lights and screens entertain flesh.

ROMANS 12:1 (KJV)

"I beseech you therefore, brethren, by the mercies of God, that ye present your bodies a living sacrifice, holy, acceptable unto God, which is your reasonable service."

The altar is for sacrifice. It is the place where men lay down their pride, their lust, their rebellion, their plans, and their flesh.

Without sacrifice, there is no fire. Without fire, there is no presence. Without presence, there is no power.

1 KINGS 18:38 (KJV)

"Then the fire of the LORD fell, and consumed the burnt sacrifice, and the wood, and the stones, and the dust, and licked up the water that was in the trench."

When Elijah rebuilt the altar, he did not put on a show. He did not need music, lights, or performance. He simply laid the sacrifice down, and God answered with fire. That is what the church is missing today: the fire that only falls when there is true sacrifice on the altar.

Instead, we have turned the altar into a stage. Preachers use it for performance. Worship teams use it for spotlight. The sacred is treated as common, and the holy as entertainment. And we wonder why there is no fire.

HEBREWS 13:10 (KJV)

"We have an altar, whereof they have no right to eat which serve the tabernacle."

The altar belongs to God alone. It is not ours to repurpose for show. It is not ours to make trendy, clever, or marketable. It is His place of sacrifice and holy fire.

Until the altar is restored, the church will remain powerless. Until repentance returns, revival will tarry. Until the fire burns again, our gatherings will be smoke without flame.

CHAPTER 6: THE ALTAR IS FOR SACRIFICE, NOT ENTERTAINMENT

TRUMPET CALL

- The altar is not a stage; it is a place of sacrifice.
- The fire of God falls only where there is death to self.
- Stop entertaining, start repenting.
- The altar must burn again with holy fire.

REFLECTION QUESTIONS

1. Do I treat the altar as a stage for performance or a place for sacrifice?
2. Have I laid down my life fully upon the altar before God?
3. Does my ministry draw applause from men or fire from heaven?
4. Is there still fire burning in my church, or only smoke?

DECLARATION

I will not treat the altar of God as common.

I will not perform where I am called to weep.

I will lay myself upon the altar daily as a living sacrifice.

I will rebuild the altar in my heart and in the house of God.

And I will not rest until the fire of God burns again upon it.

CHAPTER 7: The Gospel of the Kingdom vs. the Gospel of Success

> MATTHEW 6:33 (KJV)
>
> *"But seek ye first the kingdom of God, and his righteousness; and all these things shall be added unto you."*

The gospel of the kingdom calls us to seek God's rule first—His holiness, His will, His righteousness. But the gospel of success flips this truth upside down. Instead of seeking the kingdom, it teaches us to seek blessings, wealth, and comfort, promising that God will serve our ambitions.

This is not the gospel of Jesus Christ; it is another gospel. And Paul warned us what happens when another gospel is preached.

> GALATIANS 1:6–9 (KJV)
>
> *"I marvel that ye are so soon removed from him that called you into the grace of Christ unto another gospel:*
>
> *Which is not another; but there be some that trouble you, and would pervert the gospel of Christ.*
>
> *But though we, or an angel from heaven, preach any other gospel unto you than that which we have preached unto you, let him be accursed.*

CHAPTER 7: THE GOSPEL OF THE KINGDOM VS. THE GOSPEL OF SUCCESS

> *As we said before, so say I now again, If any man preach any other gospel unto you than that ye have received, let him be accursed."*

The gospel of success is not a small mistake; it is a perversion. It replaces the cross with cash, repentance with self-help, holiness with hype. And Paul's warning is clear: those who preach it stand under a curse, not a blessing.

LUKE 9:23 (KJV)

"And he said to them all, If any man will come after me, let him deny himself, and take up his cross daily, and follow me."

The true gospel demands denial of self. The gospel of success demands indulgence of self. One calls for a cross, the other for comfort. One produces disciples, the other produces consumers. One fills heaven, the other fills buildings but empties eternity.

And the danger is that the gospel of success looks close enough to the truth that it deceives multitudes. It still uses the name of Jesus, but strips away His demands. It still opens the Bible, but twists it to fit ambition.

PHILIPPIANS 3:18–19 (KJV)

"For many walk, of whom I have told you often, and now tell you even weeping, that they are the enemies of the cross of Christ:

Whose end is destruction, whose God is their belly, and whose glory is in their shame, who mind earthly things."

The gospel of success makes men enemies of the cross. They want a crown without a cross, glory without suffering, blessing without obedience. Their god is their belly—appetite, craving, lust for more. They glory in what should bring shame. They obsess over earthly things while neglecting the eternal.

> ### 1 Corinthians 1:18 (KJV)
>
> *"For the preaching of the cross is to them that perish foolishness; but unto us which are saved it is the power of God."*

The gospel of the kingdom is offensive. It declares that sin must die, flesh must surrender, pride must bow, and idols must fall. It demands that the old man be crucified. But the gospel of success avoids the offense. It offers a motivational speech in place of the bloody cross. It seeks applause, not repentance.

> ### Revelation 3:17 (KJV)
>
> *"Because thou sayest, I am rich, and increased with goods, and have need of nothing; and knowest not that thou art wretched, and miserable, and poor, and blind, and naked."*

This is the tragedy of the modern church: wealthy, but wretched. Full of possessions, but empty of presence. Increased with goods, but decreased in godliness. Boasting in success while blind to their own nakedness.

The gospel of success has created churches that look alive but are dead. They have confused prosperity with power, applause with anointing, and crowds with conversion.

> ### Matthew 16:24–25 (KJV)
>
> *"Then said Jesus unto his disciples, If any man will come after me, let him deny himself, and take up his cross, and follow me.*
>
> *For whosoever will save his life shall lose it: and whosoever will lose his life for my sake shall find it."*

CHAPTER 7: THE GOSPEL OF THE KINGDOM VS. THE GOSPEL OF SUCCESS

The gospel of the kingdom is costly. It calls you to lose your life to find it. It demands a daily cross, not just a Sunday service. It demands we follow Christ to Calvary, not just to convenience.

The gospel of success says: "Live your dream." The gospel of the kingdom says: "Die to yourself." One leads to hell. The other leads to eternal life.

MATTHEW 7:13-14 (KJV)

"Enter ye in at the strait gate: for wide is the gate, and broad is the way, that leadeth to destruction, and many there be which go in thereat:

Because strait is the gate, and narrow is the way, which leadeth unto life, and few there be that find it."

The gospel of success points men to the broad road—easy, attractive, popular. But Jesus said the road to life is narrow, unpopular, costly, and few will walk it.

Shepherds, beware: if your gospel is easy, it is not His gospel. If your sermons never offend the flesh, they never honor the cross.

TRUMPET CALL

- The gospel of success is not the gospel of Christ.
- Repent of preaching comfort when Christ demands a cross.
- Reject the lie that gain equals godliness.
- Return to the gospel of the kingdom—surrender, holiness, and fire.

REFLECTION QUESTIONS

1. Do I preach the cross or avoid it to please people?
2. Is my ministry built on kingdom obedience or earthly success?
3. Have I confused prosperity with the presence of God?
4. Do I measure fruit by discipleship or by numbers?
5. Would Paul recognize my message as the gospel, or call it a perversion?
6. Am I willing to lose my life daily for the sake of Christ?

DECLARATION

I renounce the gospel of success.

I will not exchange the cross for comfort, or holiness for hype.

I will preach Christ crucified, risen, and returning, even if the world mocks.

I will measure success not by numbers or applause, but by obedience to Christ.

I will seek first the kingdom of God and His righteousness, trusting Him for all else.

By His Spirit, I will bear the reproach of the cross until He comes again.

CHAPTER 8: Repentance in the House of God

1 Peter 4:17 (KJV)

"For the time is come that judgment must begin at the house of God: and if it first begin at us, what shall the end be of them that obey not the gospel of God?"

Repentance is not first a message for the world; it is a command for the church. Before God ever calls the nations to repent, He calls His people to the altar. Judgment begins in the house of God. If the pulpit is compromised, the pew will be corrupt. If the shepherds are silent, the sheep will scatter.

We cannot point our fingers at the wickedness of the world while the church refuses to fall on her face. Sin in the sanctuary is more deadly than sin in the streets. Why? Because the world sins in ignorance, but the church sins in rebellion.

2 Chronicles 7:14 (KJV)

"If my people, which are called by my name, shall humble themselves, and pray, and seek my face, and turn from their wicked ways; then will I hear from heaven, and will forgive their sin, and will heal their land."

Notice, it does not say if the world humbles itself. It says if My people do. Revival has never started with Washington; it starts with the church. Healing has never begun with politicians; it begins with the altar of God. The land will not be healed until the church is broken.

But today we are a people more concerned with appearances than repentance. We sing loud but repent little. We preach grace but rarely mention sin. We fill altars with flowers but not with tears. And we wonder why our land is sick.

ACTS 3:19 (KJV)

"Repent ye therefore, and be converted, that your sins may be blotted out, when the times of refreshing shall come from the presence of the Lord."

Refreshing only comes after repentance. We pray for revival, but we skip the step that makes revival possible. We want refreshing without repentance, power without purity, fire without brokenness. But God will not pour new wine into old wineskins. He will not send His glory where sin is protected.

If the church will repent, God will refresh. But if we refuse, He will remove His lampstand.

JAMES 4:8-10 (KJV)

"Draw nigh to God, and he will draw nigh to you. Cleanse your hands, ye sinners; and purify your hearts, ye double minded. Be afflicted, and mourn, and weep: let your laughter be turned to mourning, and your joy to heaviness. Humble yourselves in the sight of the Lord, and he shall lift you up."

The modern church has traded mourning for amusement. We laugh when we should weep. We applaud when we should tremble. We call people to celebrate when God calls them to repent. But until our laughter is turned to mourning, there will be no lifting up. Until the house of God learns to cry again, there will be no glory cloud.

> JOEL 2:12–13 (KJV)
>
> *"Therefore also now, saith the LORD, turn ye even to me with all your heart, and with fasting, and with weeping, and with mourning: And rend your heart, and not your garments, and turn unto the LORD your God: for he is gracious and merciful, slow to anger, and of great kindness, and repenteth him of the evil."*

God is not interested in outward shows of religion. He doesn't want our garments ripped in public; He wants our hearts ripped in private. True repentance is not just words spoken at an altar call; it is a heart torn open before God.

A Call to Shepherds

Shepherds, listen: the greatest need in your church is not better programs or slicker sermons. It is repentance. If you preach holiness but never call people to repentance, you have given them law without the key to life. If you preach grace but never call people to repentance, you have given them license to sin.

The sheep will not repent until the shepherds do. Pastors who have grown comfortable in compromise cannot expect their people to burn with holiness. Leaders who refuse to bow cannot expect their churches to weep. Revival will never come through pulpits that are too proud to kneel.

The Cost of Silence

The cost of refusing repentance is eternal. A church that will not repent will be judged. A pastor who refuses to repent will answer before the throne. A people that cover sin with songs will be exposed when the fire comes.

> REVELATION 2:5 (KJV)
>
> *"Remember therefore from whence thou art fallen, and repent, and do the first works; or else I will come unto thee quickly, and will remove thy candlestick out of his place, except thou repent."*

Christ's warning is not to the world but to the church. "If you do not repent, I will remove your lampstand. You may still have services. You may still have crowds. You may still have music. But you will not have Me." And without Him, we are nothing.

The Promise of Fire

The good news is this: if the church repents, God will respond. If we turn, He will heal. If we bow, He will lift us up. If we rend our hearts, He will rend the heavens.

> ISAIAH 57:15 (KJV)
>
> *"For thus saith the high and lofty One that inhabiteth eternity, whose name is Holy; I dwell in the high and holy place, with him also that is of a contrite and humble spirit, to revive the spirit of the humble, and to revive the heart of the contrite ones."*

Revival belongs to the broken. The fire of God falls not on the proud but on the contrite. If we will break, He will burn. If we will bow, He will revive.

A Cry for the Altar

Where are the tears in the house of God? Where are the wails of repentance? Where are the shepherds crying between the porch and the altar?

Until repentance returns, the altars will remain empty. Until the church is broken, the land will remain sick. Until we confess our sins, the heavens will remain brass.

But if we repent, the floodgates of heaven will open. If we weep, the fire will fall. If we humble ourselves, the Spirit will move again.

TRUMPET CALL

- Judgment begins in the house of God.
- Repentance is not optional; it is the doorway to revival.
- The land will not heal until the church bows.
- Shepherds, lead the way back to the altar.

REFLECTION QUESTIONS

1. Do I preach repentance, or do I avoid it to keep people comfortable?
2. When was the last time I wept over sin in the house of God?
3. Am I more concerned with appearance than with holiness?
4. Do my people know how to repent, or only how to sing?
5. Have I led my church in true brokenness before God?
6. Am I willing to rend my heart and let God break me?

DECLARATION

I will not protect sin in the house of God.

I will not replace repentance with entertainment.

I will call the people of God back to the altar.

I will humble myself before the Lord daily until His fire burns again.

I will preach repentance without apology, for judgment begins in the house of God.

By His Spirit, I will keep the altar burning with tears until Christ returns.

CHAPTER 9: **Ichabod and the Abandoned Altar**

1 Samuel 4:21–22 (KJV)

"And she named the child Ichabod, saying, The glory is departed from Israel: because the ark of God was taken, and because of her father in law and her husband. And she said, The glory is departed from Israel: for the ark of God is taken."

"Ichabod." One of the most tragic words in all of Scripture—"The glory has departed." Israel still had priests. They still had rituals. They still had sacrifices. But the presence was gone. And without the presence, everything else was empty.

The same danger faces the church today. We still have buildings. We still have sermons. We still have worship sets, livestreams, and conferences. But in many places, the glory has departed. The Spirit has been grieved, the altar has been forsaken, and "Ichabod" is written over the door.

Ezekiel 10:18–19 (KJV)

"Then the glory of the LORD departed from off the threshold of the house, and stood over the cherubims. And the cherubims lifted up their wings, and mounted up from the earth in my sight: when they went out, the wheels also were beside them, and every one stood at the door of the east gate of the LORD'S house; and the glory of the God of Israel was over them above."

Ezekiel saw it with his own eyes: the glory of God leaving the temple. It did not leave suddenly; it lingered at the threshold, as if waiting for repentance. But when none came, it departed.

Church, we must tremble. Do not think God is bound to our buildings. Do not think His Spirit will remain where He is unwanted. If we grieve Him long enough, He will depart. And what remains will be a form of godliness without power, religion without the presence of God.

> JEREMIAH 2:13 (KJV)
>
> *"For my people have committed two evils; they have forsaken me the fountain of living waters, and hewed them out cisterns, broken cisterns, that can hold no water."*

This is the condition of Ichabod churches. They have forsaken the fountain of living water, the Spirit of God, and they have dug out broken cisterns. They lean on human wisdom, church growth models, entertainment, and positive slogans, but none of it can hold the glory. The water runs out. The people stay thirsty. And the altar stays empty.

> REVELATION 2:4–5 (KJV)
>
> *"Nevertheless I have somewhat against thee, because thou hast left thy first love. Remember therefore from whence thou art fallen, and repent, and do the first works; or else I will come unto thee quickly, and will remove thy candlestick out of his place, except thou repent."*

Jesus warned the church of Ephesus: "You are busy, you are active, but you have abandoned your first love. And if you do not repent, I will remove your lampstand." In other words, "Your church will continue, but My presence will not be there." This is Ichabod. A church with programs, but no power. A church with crowds, but no Christ.

The Tragedy of the Abandoned Altar

The altar is the meeting place of God and man. It is the place of sacrifice, of tears, of repentance, of fire. But in many churches, the altar has been abandoned. Some removed it altogether to make more room for seats. Others replaced it with a stage. Others left it to collect dust while they turned the service into a performance.

But the altar was never meant to be a stage. It is not a place to perform; it is a place to die. The altar is where flesh is crucified, where pride is broken, where sin is confessed, where fire falls. When the altar is abandoned, so is the presence.

Shepherds Without Glory

Shepherds, hear the word of the Lord: if you abandon the altar, you abandon your calling. Your task is not to entertain but to intercede. Not to draw a crowd but to lead people to the cross. If you exchange the fire of God for the applause of man, "Ichabod" will be written over your ministry.

> EZEKIEL 22:26 (KJV)
>
> *"Her priests have violated my law, and have profaned mine holy things: they have put no difference between the holy and profane, neither have they shewed difference between the unclean and the clean, and have hid their eyes from my sabbaths, and I am profaned among them."*

This is the state of many pulpits. No difference between the holy and the profane. No distinction between clean and unclean. Entertainment in the sanctuary. Worldliness on the platform. And God says, "I am profaned among them."

The Cost of Ichabod

When the glory departs, sermons become speeches. Worship becomes noise. Baptism becomes ritual. Communion becomes snack time. Everything loses its weight because God is not in it.

We can live without fog machines. We can live without fancy lights. But we cannot live without the glory of God. And yet many churches have traded His presence for popularity. They wonder why revival tarries. They wonder why young people are leaving. They wonder why marriages are falling apart. It is because "Ichabod" has been written, and no one trembles.

The Call to Return

But hear the mercy of God: Ichabod is not the end of the story. The glory can return. The altar can be rebuilt. The presence can come back.

> HOSEA 10:12 (KJV)
>
> *"Sow to yourselves in righteousness, reap in mercy; break up your fallow ground: for it is time to seek the LORD, till he come and rain righteousness upon you."*

It is time to break up the hard ground. It is time to seek the Lord until He comes. It is time to rebuild the altar, to cry out again for His glory. If we repent, He will rain righteousness. If we return, He will restore. If we humble ourselves, the glory will come back.

CHAPTER 9: ICHABOD AND THE ABANDONED ALTAR

TRUMPET CALL

- "Ichabod" is written over churches that forsake the altar.
- The glory departs where sin is excused and holiness is mocked.
- The altar is not a stage; it is a place of fire and sacrifice.
- Return to your first love, and the glory will return.

REFLECTION QUESTIONS

1. Has "Ichabod" been written over my life, ministry, or church?
2. Have I abandoned the altar for a stage?
3. Do I know the difference between activity and anointing?
4. Is the glory of God truly present in our gatherings?
5. What broken cisterns have I trusted instead of the fountain of living water?
6. Am I willing to rebuild the altar with tears, repentance, and prayer?

DECLARATION

I will not live with "Ichabod" written over my life.

I will not exchange the presence of God for popularity.

I will return to the altar, to repentance, to brokenness.

I will guard the glory of God above all else.

By His mercy, I will seek His face until His fire falls again.

The altar will not be abandoned; it will burn with sacrifice until Jesus comes.

CHAPTER 10: The Compromised Pulpit and the Silenced Prophets

> ISAIAH 58:1 (KJV)
>
> *"Cry aloud, spare not, lift up thy voice like a trumpet, and shew my people their transgression, and the house of Jacob their sins."*

The pulpit was never meant to be safe. It was never meant to be a place for smooth words and flattering speech. It was meant to be a place where God's word thunders like a trumpet, cutting through sin, exposing darkness, and calling men to repentance. But today, too many pulpits are compromised. Too many prophets are silent. And the people are perishing because no one dares to cry aloud anymore.

> JEREMIAH 23:16–17 (KJV)
>
> *"Thus saith the LORD of hosts, Hearken not unto the words of the prophets that prophesy unto you: they make you vain: they speak a vision of their own heart, and not out of the mouth of the LORD. They say still unto them that despise me, The LORD hath said, Ye shall have peace; and they say unto every one that walketh after the imagination of his own heart, No evil shall come upon you."*

CHAPTER 10: THE COMPROMISED PULPIT AND THE SILENCED PROPHETS

This is the sound of the modern pulpit—peace, peace, when there is no peace. Messages of comfort without conviction. Promises of blessing without obedience. Smooth sermons that soothe the flesh but never pierce the heart. And God says, "They make you vain."

The greatest danger to the church is not atheism in the streets; it is false prophecy in the pulpit.

> EZEKIEL 33:6–7 (KJV)
>
> *"But if the watchman see the sword come, and blow not the trumpet, and the people be not warned; if the sword come, and take any person from among them, he is taken away in his iniquity; but his blood will I require at the watchman's hand. So thou, O son of man, I have set thee a watchman unto the house of Israel; therefore thou shalt hear the word at my mouth, and warn them from me."*

Shepherd, prophet, pastor, if you refuse to warn, you will answer for the blood of your people. If you see sin and stay silent, God will require it of you. To stand in the pulpit and entertain while the sword is at the door is spiritual negligence of the highest order.

The watchman who refuses to sound the alarm is guilty of murder. And pulpits across this land are filled with guilty watchmen who will not blow the trumpet.

> MICAH 3:11 (KJV)
>
> *"The heads thereof judge for reward, and the priests thereof teach for hire, and the prophets thereof divine for money: yet will they lean upon the LORD, and say, Is not the LORD among us? none evil can come upon us."*

This is the gospel of the compromised pulpit. Preach for hire. Prophesy for money. Teach for applause. Build your brand. Grow your influence. And then claim God is with you. But God says:

"Ichabod." The glory is departed. You may have a following, but you do not have fire. You may have fans, but you do not have the fear of the Lord.

2 Timothy 4:2–4 (KJV)

"Preach the word; be instant in season, out of season; reprove, rebuke, exhort with all longsuffering and doctrine. For the time will come when they will not endure sound doctrine; but after their own lusts shall they heap to themselves teachers, having itching ears; And they shall turn away their ears from the truth, and shall be turned unto fables."

That time is here. People no longer want sound doctrine; they want motivational speeches. They no longer want truth; they want fables. They no longer want prophets; they want performers. And instead of resisting, the pulpits have complied. Instead of rebuking sin, they reinforce it. Instead of reproving rebellion, they bless it.

The result? Churches filled with people, but empty of God. Congregations applauding sermons that God never spoke. Prophets silenced by fear of man. Shepherds fattening sheep for slaughter instead of leading them to holiness.

The Sin of Silence

Silence is not neutrality. It is complicity. When the pulpit refuses to speak against sin, it gives sin permission to thrive. When prophets refuse to confront wickedness, the people assume God is pleased.

The compromised pulpit does not say, "Go sin." It simply refuses to say, "Repent." And the result is the same: people perish.

Lamentations 2:14 (KJV)

"Thy prophets have seen vain and foolish things for thee: and they have not discovered thine iniquity, to turn away

thy captivity; but have seen for thee false burdens and causes of banishment."

The prophets failed because they would not expose sin. They wanted to encourage without confronting. They wanted to uplift without uprooting. But a gospel without repentance cannot save. It is spiritual malpractice to give people hope without holiness.

The Cost of Compromise

When pulpits are compromised, nations collapse. When prophets are silent, sin reigns. The church loses its salt. The light grows dim. The enemy advances unchecked.

And God holds the watchmen responsible. The blood is on their hands.

A Call to the True Prophets

But God still has a remnant. He still has watchmen who refuse to bow. He still has prophets who will weep between the porch and the altar. He still has shepherds who tremble at His word and will not be bought.

> JEREMIAH 20:9 (KJV)
>
> *"Then I said, I will not make mention of him, nor speak any more in his name. But his word was in mine heart as a burning fire shut up in my bones, and I was weary with forbearing, and I could not stay."*

This is the mark of a true prophet—the fire of God burning in their bones. They cannot stay silent. They cannot compromise. They cannot dilute the word. They may be mocked, rejected, persecuted, or even killed, but they cannot stop speaking what God has said.

The Promise of Fire

If the pulpits will repent of compromise, if the prophets will rise again, if the watchmen will blow the trumpet, God will send fire once more. Revival is not born in silence; it is born in bold proclamation of truth. The early church turned the world upside down not with entertainment but with unshakable preaching of repentance, the cross, the resurrection, and the coming judgment.

If we want that power again, we must return to that pulpit. A pulpit on fire. A pulpit unyielding. A pulpit unashamed.

CHAPTER 10: THE COMPROMISED PULPIT AND THE SILENCED PROPHETS

TRUMPET CALL

- ✥ Compromise in the pulpit is treason against heaven.
- ✥ A silent prophet is as deadly as a false prophet.
- ✥ Shepherds, blow the trumpet; sin must be named and judged.
- ✥ Preach the word, in season and out, even if the world rejects it.

REFLECTION QUESTIONS

1. Do I preach the whole counsel of God, or only what people want to hear?
2. Have I avoided hard truths to protect my position or reputation?
3. Am I a watchman who blows the trumpet, or one who stays silent?
4. Do I fear man more than I fear God?
5. Has the fire of God's word burned in my bones, or have I silenced it?
6. Am I willing to preach repentance even if it costs me everything?

DECLARATION

I renounce compromise in the pulpit.

I will not water down God's word to please men.

I will preach repentance, righteousness, and holiness without apology.

I will not be silent when sin must be confronted.

The word of God will burn in my bones, and I will cry aloud like a trumpet.

By His Spirit, I will stand as a watchman until Christ returns.

CHAPTER 11: The Great Falling Away Has Already Begun

2 Thessalonians 2:3 (KJV)

"Let no man deceive you by any means: for that day shall not come, except there come a falling away first, and that man of sin be revealed, the son of perdition."

The apostle Paul warned of a great falling away before the return of Christ. Not a falling away of the world, but of the church. Not the rebellion of atheists, but the apostasy of those who once claimed His name. And today, we can no longer speak of this falling away as a future event. It is already here.

Look around. The signs are everywhere. Churches once ablaze with truth now wink at sin. Leaders once trembling before God now tremble before culture. What Paul called the "falling away" is happening in our pulpits, in our pews, in our homes. Apostasy is not coming. Apostasy has arrived.

1 Timothy 4:1–2 (KJV)

"Now the Spirit speaketh expressly, that in the latter times some shall depart from the faith, giving heed to seducing spirits, and doctrines of devils; Speaking lies in hypocrisy; having their conscience seared with a hot iron."

CHAPTER 11: THE GREAT FALLING AWAY HAS ALREADY BEGUN

This is the age we are living in. Seducing spirits fill the pulpits. Doctrines of devils are packaged as positive sermons. Consciences are seared. Sin is celebrated. Rebellion is excused. The faith is being abandoned not by outsiders, but by insiders. By pastors, leaders, and believers who once confessed Christ but have now traded truth for deception.

MATTHEW 24:10–12 (KJV)

"And then shall many be offended, and shall betray one another, and shall hate one another. And many false prophets shall rise, and shall deceive many. And because iniquity shall abound, the love of many shall wax cold."

Offense is everywhere. Hatred has entered the pews. False prophets rise on every corner, and deception spreads like wildfire. Iniquity abounds, not just in the world, but in the house of God. And the love of many has grown cold.

This is not a distant prophecy. It is a present reality. The great falling away is now.

HEBREWS 3:12 (KJV)

"Take heed, brethren, lest there be in any of you an evil heart of unbelief, in departing from the living God."

This is not about unbelievers. It is about brethren. Those who once walked with Christ, who once prayed, who once sang, who once believed, but now are departing. Drifting. Falling. Apostasy does not always look like open rebellion. Sometimes, it looks like slow compromise, little by little, until Christ is no longer Lord, but just a label.

2 PETER 2:1–2 (KJV)

"But there were false prophets also among the people, even as there shall be false teachers among you, who privily

> *shall bring in damnable heresies, even denying the Lord that bought them, and bring upon themselves swift destruction. And many shall follow their pernicious ways; by reason of whom the way of truth shall be evil spoken of.*

False teachers are not rare; they are many. And "many shall follow them." This is the tragedy of apostasy. It is not just that leaders fall. It is that multitudes follow. The way of truth is evil spoken of because of those who once claimed to preach it.

Signs of the Falling Away

- Truth traded for tolerance. Pastors more afraid of offending men than offending God.
- Holiness mocked. Those who pursue purity are labeled extreme.
- Sin blessed. Rebellion called freedom, immorality called love.
- Comfort over the cross. Sermons promising ease, never repentance.
- Deception rising. Smooth words replacing fire. Popularity replacing power.
- Cold love. Believers so consumed with self that they can no longer love God or neighbor.

This is the evidence that apostasy is here.

The Cost of Apostasy

The cost of this great falling away is eternal. Multitudes who think they are saved will stand before Christ and hear, "I never knew you." Churches that look alive will be spewed out of His mouth. Leaders who silenced repentance will answer for the blood of their people.

Apostasy damns souls. It fills hell. It turns the church into a powerless shell. And the judgment of God is already at the door.

But not all will fall. God has always preserved a remnant. Even when Israel bowed to Baal, there were seven thousand who did not. Even when the priests grew corrupt, God raised up prophets who refused to be silent.

Jude 1:3 (KJV)

"Beloved, when I gave all diligence to write unto you of the common salvation, it was needful for me to write unto you, and exhort you that ye should earnestly contend for the faith which was once delivered unto the saints."

This is our call in the hour of apostasy to contend for the faith. To refuse compromise. To hold fast to the word. To endure hatred, rejection, persecution, and still stand.

Hope in the Remnant

The falling away is real. It is widespread. But it is not the end of the story. God has a remnant who refuse to bow. A people who will not trade truth for lies. A church within the church that still burns for holiness, still loves the word, still trembles at His presence.

If you are reading these words and feel the Spirit stirring you, do not harden your heart. Do not drift with the crowd. Do not bow to Baal. Stand. Contend. Be counted among the remnant.

TRUMPET CALL

- The great falling away is not coming; it is here.
- Apostasy is not outside the church, but inside.
- Many are departing, but God is raising a remnant.
- Contend for the faith, even if the world mocks.

REFLECTION QUESTIONS

1. Am I drifting slowly away from the truth without realizing it?
2. Have I traded conviction for comfort?
3. Do I recognize the signs of apostasy in my church, family, or life?
4. Am I willing to be hated for standing with Christ?
5. Have I contended for the faith, or gone along with the crowd?
6. Am I part of the remnant who will endure to the end?

DECLARATION

I will not fall away.

I will not trade truth for tolerance, or holiness for hype.

I will stand in this evil day, clothed in the armor of God.

I will contend for the faith once delivered to the saints.

Though many depart, I will remain faithful by His Spirit.

I will endure to the end, and by His grace, I will see His face.

CHAPTER 12: **Woe to the Shameless Shepherds**

Ezekiel 34:2-4 (KJV)

"Son of man, prophesy against the shepherds of Israel, prophesy, and say unto them, Thus saith the Lord GOD unto the shepherds; Woe be to the shepherds of Israel that do feed themselves! should not the shepherds feed the flocks? Ye eat the fat, and ye clothe you with the wool, ye kill them that are fed: but ye feed not the flock. The diseased have ye not strengthened, neither have ye healed that which was sick, neither have ye bound up that which was broken, neither have ye brought again that which was driven away, neither have ye sought that which was lost; but with force and with cruelty have ye ruled them."

God's fiercest rebukes in Scripture are not against the drunkards, thieves, or pagans, but against the shepherds who betrayed His flock. These shepherds were called to feed, protect, and care for the sheep, but instead, they fed themselves. They clothed themselves with the wool of the sheep while leaving the sheep naked, sick, broken, and lost. And God's verdict over them is one word: "Woe."

Jeremiah 23:1-2 (KJV)

"Woe be unto the pastors that destroy and scatter the sheep of my pasture! saith the LORD. Therefore thus saith

the LORD God of Israel against the pastors that feed my people; Ye have scattered my flock, and driven them away, and have not visited them: behold, I will visit upon you the evil of your doings, saith the LORD."

The pulpit is not a platform for self-promotion. It is not a stage for ambition. It is not a means to wealth. It is a sacred trust to feed the flock of God. Yet many have destroyed and scattered the sheep. They build empires while the sheep starve. They grow brands while the sheep bleed. And God promises: He will visit them in judgment.

ZECHARIAH 11:17 (KJV)

"Woe to the idol shepherd that leaveth the flock! the sword shall be upon his arm, and upon his right eye: his arm shall be clean dried up, and his right eye shall be utterly darkened."

The idle shepherd leaves the sheep to fend for themselves. He does not care when they wander. He does not grieve when they fall. He does not fight when the wolves come. He is content to collect the benefits of the title while neglecting the burden of the call. But God declares woe—judgment against the idle shepherd who abandons the flock.

JOHN 10:12–13 (KJV)

"But he that is an hireling, and not the shepherd, whose own the sheep are not, seeth the wolf coming, and leaveth the sheep, and fleeth: and the wolf catcheth them, and scattereth the sheep. The hireling fleeth, because he is an hireling, and careth not for the sheep."

The shameless shepherd is a hireling. He is in ministry for a paycheck, not a cross. For applause, not sacrifice. When the wolves

CHAPTER 12: WOE TO THE SHAMELESS SHEPHERDS

come—when sin must be confronted, when culture presses in, when persecution rises—he flees. He abandons the sheep because his heart was never for the sheep, but for himself.

ISAIAH 56:10–11 (KJV)

"His watchmen are blind: they are all ignorant, they are all dumb dogs, they cannot bark; sleeping, lying down, loving to slumber. Yea, they are greedy dogs which can never have enough, and they are shepherds that cannot understand: they all look to their own way, every one for his gain, from his quarter."

What a picture of our pulpits today: blind watchmen, dumb dogs who cannot bark, greedy shepherds who never have enough. They measure success in offerings, numbers, and applause, not in holiness, repentance, or the fear of the Lord. They are shameless—preaching without weeping, leading without sacrifice, demanding honor without giving it.

The Shamelessness of the Modern Pulpit

Shameless shepherds do not blush at sin. They laugh at holiness. They boast in their brand while their sheep wander into destruction. They preach feel-good messages while marriages collapse, while addictions thrive, while sin goes unchallenged. They are not burdened. They are not broken. They are not trembling before the word of God. They are shameless.

And when there is no shame in the shepherd, there will be no repentance in the flock.

The Woe of God

When God says "Woe," it is not a suggestion. It is a sentence. It is a divine declaration of judgment. The shameless shepherd may live in ease now, but judgment is coming. God Himself says He will remove them from feeding the flock, and He will require His sheep at their hand (Ezek 34:10).

This is why James warned: "My brethren, be not many masters, knowing that we shall receive the greater condemnation" (Jas 3:1). To stand in the pulpit is to invite stricter judgment. And to abuse that pulpit is to invite the wrath of Almighty God.

The Wounded Flock

What happens when shepherds are shameless? The sheep scatter. They starve. They are devoured by wolves. They wander without direction. Instead of being led beside still waters, they are led into confusion. Instead of being fed the Bread of Life, they are fed crumbs of entertainment. Instead of being healed, they are abandoned.

And many sheep, wounded by false shepherds, now despise all shepherds. Many souls, betrayed by corrupt pastors, now despise the very name of Christ. This is the devastating cost of shameless shepherds.

The True Shepherd

But thanks be to God, there is still a Good Shepherd. His name is Jesus Christ. He does not fleece the flock; He laid down His life for the flock. He does not abandon in the face of wolves; He crushed the head of the serpent. He does not feed Himself; He feeds us with His own body and blood.

The shameless shepherd seeks his own glory. The Good Shepherd seeks the salvation of His sheep. The shameless shepherd runs when danger comes. The Good Shepherd runs toward the danger and gives His life.

And God is raising up shepherds after His own heart—men who tremble at His word, who weep over sin, who lay down their lives in prayer, fasting, and sacrifice for the flock of God.

The Call to Repentance

Shepherds, hear the word of the Lord: repent. Return to the altar. Return to tears. Return to the call. Stop feeding yourselves. Stop fleecing the flock. Stop hiding from the wolves. God is calling for shepherds who will lead in holiness, courage, and sacrifice.

If you have been shameless, repent before the shame of judgment falls. If you have abandoned the flock, return before God removes you. If you have mocked holiness, tremble before the fire consumes you.

The hour is late. The sheep are bleeding. The wolves are circling. And God is saying once more: "Woe to the shameless shepherds."

TRUMPET CALL

- Woe to the shepherds who feed themselves and neglect the flock.
- God will hold accountable those who scatter and wound His sheep.
- The pulpit is not a stage for ambition, but an altar of sacrifice.
- Return to the call, repent of shamelessness, and follow the Good Shepherd.

REFLECTION QUESTIONS

1. Am I feeding the flock or feeding myself?
2. Do I weep over sin, or laugh at it?
3. Have I abandoned the altar for ambition?
4. Do I tremble at God's word, or treat it lightly?
5. Am I a shepherd after God's heart, or a hireling chasing gain?
6. Will the flock under me be found healthy, holy, and ready when Christ returns?

DECLARATION

I renounce shamelessness in the pulpit.

I will not fleece the flock; I will feed the flock.

I will not run from the wolves; I will stand and fight for the sheep.

I will not seek my own glory; I will glorify the Good Shepherd.

By His Spirit, I will be a shepherd after His heart, willing to lay down my life for His people.

The sheep are His, the call is His, and to Him alone be the glory.

CHAPTER 13: The Rise of the Remnant Watchmen

ROMANS 11:4–5 (KJV)

"But what saith the answer of God unto him? I have reserved to myself seven thousand men, who have not bowed the knee to the image of Baal. Even so then at this present time also there is a remnant according to the election of grace."

Elijah thought he was alone. He thought every prophet had bowed, every voice had gone silent, every watchman had abandoned the wall. But God reminded him that there is always a remnant. A hidden company. A faithful few. A people who refuse to bow, refuse to compromise, refuse to let the fire go out.

And so it is today. Though pulpits are polluted and shepherds are shameless, God has reserved for Himself a remnant. They are not the celebrities. They are not the popular preachers. They are the nameless, faceless servants of God who will not bow to Baal, who will not sell out, who will not go silent. They are the remnant watchmen rising in this hour.

ISAIAH 62:6 (KJV)

"I have set watchmen upon thy walls, O Jerusalem, which shall never hold their peace day nor night: ye that make mention of the LORD, keep not silence."

TO THE SHEPHERDS

This is the calling of the watchman: to never hold their peace. To cry aloud day and night. To refuse silence while sin destroys, while deception spreads, while the sheep scatter. The remnant watchmen are not silent men; they are trumpet voices. Their words are not polished to please men, but sharpened to pierce hearts.

The world has enough performers. Heaven is raising watchmen.

EZEKIEL 22:30 (KJV)

"And I sought for a man among them, that should make up the hedge, and stand in the gap before me for the land, that I should not destroy it: but I found none."

What a tragedy! God searched for a man to stand, and He found none. But in our day, God is finding some. Not many. Not the majority. But some. A remnant. Those who will stand in the gap when others flee. Those who will risk their reputation, their pulpits, even their lives, to intercede for a perishing people.

The remnant are not the ones seeking applause. They are the ones weeping between the porch and the altar.

JOEL 2:17 (KJV)

"Let the priests, the ministers of the LORD, weep between the porch and the altar, and let them say, Spare thy people, O LORD, and give not thine heritage to reproach, that the heathen should rule over them: wherefore should they say among the people, Where is their God?"

The shameless shepherds joke on stage, but the remnant priests weep on their faces. The compromised entertain the crowd, but the watchmen cry out to God. The remnant understands: revival is not birthed in smoke machines and lights, but in tears and travail. The rise of the remnant is not about charisma; it is about consecration.

CHAPTER 13: THE RISE OF THE REMNANT WATCHMEN

ACTS 4:19-20 (KJV)

"But Peter and John answered and said unto them, Whether it be right in the sight of God to hearken unto you more than unto God, judge ye. For we cannot but speak the things which we have seen and heard."

This is the spirit of the remnant. They cannot be silenced. They cannot be bought. They cannot be manipulated. They cannot be threatened into silence. Like Jeremiah, the word of God burns in their bones, and they cannot hold it in. They will speak if it costs them their position, their platform, their freedom, even their lives.

The Contrast

While shameless shepherds feed themselves, remnant watchmen feed the sheep.

While false prophets say "peace, peace," the remnant warns of judgment.

While hirelings run when the wolves come, the remnant stand and fight.

While the masses bow to Baal, the remnant bow only to Christ.

The falling away is real, but so is the rising up. The remnants are emerging.

The Cost of the Remnant

The remnant will not be applauded. They will be hated, mocked, misunderstood, and rejected. They will be accused of being divisive, extreme, judgmental, or outdated. But they will not care because they fear God more than they fear man.

They may lose pulpits, but they will gain power. They may lose followers, but they will gain fire. They may lose their lives, but they will gain a crown.

The Power of the Remnant

God will anoint His remnant with authority. While others speak empty words, their words will pierce. While others build empires, they will build altars. While others chase relevance, they will carry revival. They may not look impressive to men, but they will shake nations in the Spirit.

The remnants are not many, but they are mighty because God is with them.

The Call to the Reader

The question is not whether a remnant exists. The question is whether you will be part of it. Will you rise, or will you bow? Will you contend, or will you compromise? Will you be silent, or will you sound the trumpet?

The remnant is rising. The watchmen are taking their posts. The wall is being manned again. The only question left is: will you join them?

TRUMPET CALL

- God has always preserved a remnant, and they are rising now.
- Watchmen, take your posts. Refuse silence. Blow the trumpet.
- The hour is late, the wall is broken, but God is raising voices.
- Be counted among the faithful who will not bow to Baal.

REFLECTION QUESTIONS

1. Am I living as part of the crowd, or as part of the remnant?
2. Do I remain silent when God is calling me to speak?
3. Have I bowed to Baal—to culture, compromise, or fear?
4. Am I willing to be hated, mocked, or rejected for standing as a watchman?
5. Does God's word burn in my bones, or has my fire gone out?
6. Will I rise and take my post on the wall in this final hour?

DECLARATION

I will not bow to Baal.

I will not go silent when God has called me to speak.

I will take my place among the remnant, standing in the gap, blowing the trumpet.

Though others may fall away, I will endure to the end by His Spirit.

I will live as a watchman on the wall until my King returns.

CHAPTER 14: Merchandising the Anointing

2 Peter 2:3 (KJV)

"And through covetousness shall they with feigned words make merchandise of you: whose judgment now of a long time lingereth not, and their damnation slumbereth not."

The apostle Peter warned us plainly that false teachers would come, driven by greed, using smooth words to make merchandise of God's people. The flock of God, purchased with the blood of Christ, would be turned into customers. The house of prayer would be turned into a marketplace. And Peter thundered that judgment was already on the way.

This is the hour we are living in. The anointing is no longer regarded as holy oil; it is bottled and sold like a product. Prophecy is auctioned to the highest bidder. Worship is marketed like entertainment. Sermons are crafted to secure donations, not to secure repentance. This is merchandising the anointing, and it is an abomination to the Lord.

Acts 8:18–20 (KJV)

"And when Simon saw that through laying on of the apostles' hands the Holy Ghost was given, he offered them money, Saying, Give me also this power, that on whomsoever I lay hands, he may receive the Holy Ghost. But Peter

said unto him, Thy money perish with thee, because thou hast thought that the gift of God may be purchased with money."

From the very beginning, the Spirit of God made it clear: the anointing is not for sale. When Simon the sorcerer tried to buy the power of the Holy Ghost, Peter did not negotiate with him. He rebuked him with fire: "Thy money perish with thee!" That same word needs to echo today into pulpits that have turned the oil of God into merchandise.

The gifts of God cannot be purchased. The power of God cannot be sold. The anointing cannot be franchised. It is holy, and those who attempt to profit from it bring damnation upon themselves.

MICAH 3:11 (KJV)

"The heads thereof judge for reward, and the priests thereof teach for hire, and the prophets thereof divine for money: yet will they lean upon the LORD, and say, Is not the LORD among us? none evil can come upon us."

Micah saw it in his day as prophets were prophesying for a price, priests teaching only when paid, and leaders judging for reward. And yet, they dared to claim the presence of the Lord was with them. God declared woe upon such leaders, for they took His name in vain while prostituting His word.

Is this not what we see now? Ministries turned into corporations. Pastors demanding salaries fit for kings while their people live in poverty. Conferences that charge admission for access to "anointed" messages. This is not the gospel of Christ; it is the merchandising of the anointing.

MATTHEW 21:12-13 (KJV)

"And Jesus went into the temple of God, and cast out all them that sold and bought in the temple, and overthrew

the tables of the moneychangers, and the seats of them that sold doves, And said unto them, It is written, My house shall be called the house of prayer; but ye have made it a den of thieves."

If Jesus walked into many of our churches today, He would not applaud the programs or the offerings. He would flip the tables. He would drive out the sellers of holy things. He would thunder again: "My house shall be called a house of prayer; but ye have made it a den of thieves."

We think we are safe because we attach His name to our marketing. We stamp Bible verses on our merchandise and convince ourselves that it is ministry. But if the goal is gain and not godliness, we are thieves in His house.

1 Timothy 6:5 (KJV)

"Perverse disputings of men of corrupt minds, and destitute of the truth, supposing that gain is godliness: from such withdraw thyself."

The modern gospel of greed teaches that wealth is the proof of God's favor. It equates gain with godliness. But Paul told Timothy to withdraw from such men, not to platform them. When money becomes the measure of ministry, corruption has already set in.

The true gospel calls us to deny self, to take up the cross, to give freely as we have received. The merchandising gospel calls us to indulge self, to take up ambition, to sell what was given without cost. The two are not the same. One leads to life; the other leads to damnation.

The Sin of Merchandising

Merchandising the anointing takes many forms:
- Selling "miracle water" or "prayer cloths" for a price.
- Manipulating offerings with promises God never spoke.
- Turning worship into an industry, where songs are written for sales, not souls.
- Preaching only when the honorarium is high enough.
- Treating the sacred pulpit like a stage to market personality instead of proclaiming truth.

This is not ministry. It is manipulation. It is witchcraft draped in Christian language. It is the desecration of the holy.

The Woe of God

The Lord will not remain silent. Just as Jesus overturned the tables, He will overturn pulpits built on greed. Just as He rebuked Simon the sorcerer, He will rebuke shepherds who have sold His name. Just as He declared woe through Micah, He will declare woe again today.

Judgment will begin in the house of God. Those who merchandise His anointing will face His wrath. He will strip them of their platforms, expose their corruption, and reclaim His name from their abuse.

The Contrast

The apostles refused to merchandise the gospel. Paul worked with his own hands so he would not burden the flock. They preached freely, suffered willingly, and gave everything without cost. The true anointing is always marked by sacrifice, never by sales.

The Spirit is grieved by merchandising. But He is pleased when His servants minister freely, weeping, praying, fasting, and pouring out their lives with no thought of return. This is the way of the cross, not the way of commerce.

The Call

Church, it is time to cleanse the temple again. Tear down the marketing of the holy. Refuse the merchandised gospel. Return to the house of prayer, to the purity of ministry, to the fire of freely given anointing.

To every shepherd who has sold what is sacred: repent. To every prophet who has prophesied for a price: repent. To every singer who has turned worship into performance: repent. The Spirit is calling for cleansing. The anointing is not for sale.

CHAPTER 14: MERCHANDISING THE ANOINTING

TRUMPET CALL

- The anointing is not for sale; it is holy.
- God's house is a house of prayer, not a marketplace.
- Those who merchandise the gospel bring judgment on themselves.
- Return to purity, to prayer, and to freely given ministry.

REFLECTION QUESTIONS

1. Have I treated the things of God as merchandise rather than as holy?
2. Do I measure success by offerings and sales, or by obedience and holiness?
3. Have I ever sold what God intended to be given freely?
4. Would Jesus overturn my table, or would He find me faithful?
5. Am I willing to minister without pay, trusting God to provide?
6. Do I see the anointing as sacred, or as a means to success?

DECLARATION

I renounce the merchandising of the anointing.

I will not sell what God has given freely.

I will not make merchandise of the flock of God.

I will preach, pray, and minister for His glory, not for profit.

I will guard the holiness of His presence and treat His anointing as sacred.

My ministry will not be a den of thieves, but a house of prayer.

The anointing is holy, and it belongs to Him alone.

CHAPTER 15: The Hirelings Who Scattered My Sheep

JOHN 10:12–13 (KJV)

"But he that is an hireling, and not the shepherd, whose own the sheep are not, seeth the wolf coming, and leaveth the sheep, and fleeth: and the wolf catcheth them, and scattereth the sheep. The hireling fleeth, because he is an hireling, and careth not for the sheep."

Jesus drew the line with piercing clarity: there are true shepherds, and there are hirelings. Shepherds stay when danger comes. Hirelings run. Shepherds fight for the sheep. Hirelings fight for themselves. The difference is love; one lays down his life, the other saves his own skin.

And because cowardly leaders flee, the sheep are left defenseless. Wolves rush in. The flock scatters. Souls are lost. And the name of Christ is mocked before the world.

JEREMIAH 23:1–2 (KJV)

"Woe be unto the pastors that destroy and scatter the sheep of my pasture! saith the LORD. Therefore thus saith the LORD God of Israel against the pastors that feed my people; Ye have scattered my flock, and driven them away, and have not visited them: behold, I will visit upon you the evil of your doings, saith the LORD."

CHAPTER 15: THE HIRELINGS WHO SCATTERED MY SHEEP

This is not man's complaint; it is God's accusation. The Lord Himself charges pastors with scattering His flock. They did not feed them. They did not visit them. They did not care for them. And God declares plainly: "I will visit upon you the evil of your doings."

The blood of scattered sheep cries out from the ground, and God hears it.

> ZECHARIAH 11:17 (KJV)
>
> *"Woe to the idol shepherd that leaveth the flock! the sword shall be upon his arm, and upon his right eye: his arm shall be clean dried up, and his right eye shall be utterly darkened."*

The idle shepherd, the one who leaves the flock, is under a sword of judgment. His strength withers. His vision fails. This is God's decree against those who abandon His people. He does not call them shepherds; He calls them idols. Empty. Powerless. Worthless.

False shepherds don't just fail to lead; they actively abandon. They leave the sheep wandering, confused, and broken. And the Lord swears His judgment will cut them down.

> EZEKIEL 34:10 (KJV)
>
> *"Thus saith the Lord GOD; Behold, I am against the shepherds; and I will require my flock at their hand, and cause them to cease from feeding the flock; neither shall the shepherds feed themselves any more; for I will deliver my flock from their mouth, that they may not be meat for them."*

God does not sit idly by. He says, "I am against the shepherds." He Himself will remove them. He Himself will deliver His flock. The sheep belong to Him, not to men who use them for gain. And when leaders scatter and devour, the Lord will intervene with fierce judgment.

TO THE SHEPHERDS

MATTHEW 9:36 (KJV)

"But when he saw the multitudes, he was moved with compassion on them, because they fainted, and were scattered abroad, as sheep having no shepherd."

This is the heart of Christ. While impostors scatter, He gathers. While leaders abandon, He has compassion. While pulpits run, the Good Shepherd draws near. Jesus lays down His life for the sheep—something no cowardly hireling would ever do.

This is the contrast. Self-serving pastors destroy. Christ restores. False shepherds scatter. Christ gathers. Abandoners flee. Christ remains.

The Tragedy of Scattered Sheep

The greatest cost of false shepherds is not in the pulpit; it is in the pews. Scattered sheep wander into deception, despair, and destruction. Some leave the faith altogether, not because Christ failed them, but because His so-called shepherds did. They were starved of truth, abandoned in crisis, left without protection, and they fell prey to wolves.

The cowardice of leaders becomes the ruin of souls.

The Woe of God

God's wrath burns against this betrayal. He promises to hold unfaithful leaders accountable for every scattered soul. The pulpits that scatter will face the judgment throne. Those who abandoned the sheep will face the Lion of Judah. The hirelings who run will find no escape when the Chief Shepherd comes.

The Call to True Shepherds

But even as He rebukes hirelings, God is raising up faithful shepherds. Men and women after His heart, who will feed His flock, guard them from wolves, and weep for their souls. Leaders who will not count their lives dear, but will lay them down for the sake of the sheep. Watchmen who will not run, but who will fight on their knees until victory comes.

This is the call: reject the way of the false shepherd and embrace the way of the cross. Love the sheep as Christ loved them, even unto death.

TRUMPET CALL

- Woe to the hirelings who scatter the flock; the Lord is against you.
- True shepherds, feed the sheep, bind up the broken, seek the lost.
- The flock belongs to God, not to you.
- Stand firm when the wolves come, even unto death.

REFLECTION QUESTIONS

1. Have I acted like a hireling, abandoning when the cost was high?
2. Do I love the sheep, or only what I gain from them?
3. Am I willing to stand against wolves, even if it costs me?
4. Have I scattered anyone through negligence or compromise?
5. Am I shepherding with Christ's compassion, or with self-interest?
6. On judgment day, will God call me a faithful shepherd or a hireling?

DECLARATION

I renounce the way of the hireling.

I will not abandon the flock entrusted to me.

I will not flee when the wolves come.

I will feed, guard, and love the sheep with the heart of Christ.

By the Spirit's power, I will stand my ground, even unto death.

I belong to the Good Shepherd, and I will reflect His love and courage.

CHAPTER 16: **A Church Without Conviction**

> JOHN 16:8 (KJV)
>
> *"And when he is come, he will reprove the world of sin, and of righteousness, and of judgment."*

The Holy Ghost was not sent to entertain us, flatter us, or make us comfortable in our sin. He was sent to convict—to pierce hearts with the truth of God, to strip away excuses, and to bring us face-to-face with our desperate need for Christ. Without conviction, there is no repentance. Without repentance, there is no salvation. And without salvation, there is no church: only a gathering of people with no glory.

Yet in this generation, conviction has gone missing. The modern church has traded fiery preaching for flattering words, piercing truth for polished speeches, and the sharp sword of the Spirit for the soft pillows of compromise.

> 2 TIMOTHY 4:3–4 (KJV)
>
> *"For the time will come when they will not endure sound doctrine; but after their own lusts shall they heap to themselves teachers, having itching ears; And they shall turn away their ears from the truth, and shall be turned unto fables."*

Paul warned of this day, and it has arrived. People no longer endure sound doctrine. They do not want sermons that cut to the heart; they want speeches that scratch their ears. They do not want to be called to repentance; they want to be reassured in rebellion. They do not want holiness; they want hype. And pulpits across the land have bent to this demand.

But a gospel without conviction is no gospel at all. A sermon that never pierces never saves. A church that avoids offense avoids obedience.

Hebrews 4:12 (KJV)

"For the word of God is quick, and powerful, and sharper than any twoedged sword, piercing even to the dividing asunder of soul and spirit, and of the joints and marrow, and is a discerner of the thoughts and intents of the heart."

The word of God was never meant to be dull. It was never meant to be sanitized, softened, or stripped of its power. It is a sword—sharp, piercing, cutting. It divides between truth and error, righteousness and sin, flesh and Spirit. When the word is preached in the fire of the Spirit, it convicts. It makes sinners cry out, "What must I do to be saved?"

But today's pulpits wield butter knives instead of swords. Messages are carefully crafted to avoid offense. The sharp edge is dulled. The piercing truth is replaced with positive affirmations. The result? People sit in pews every Sunday, applauded on their way to hell.

Acts 2:37 (KJV)

"Now when they heard this, they were pricked in their heart, and said unto Peter and to the rest of the apostles, Men and brethren, what shall we do?"

CHAPTER 16: A CHURCH WITHOUT CONVICTION

This is true preaching. When Peter stood up on the day of Pentecost, he did not entertain the crowd; he convicted them. He declared the cross. He confronted sin. And the people were cut to the heart. Conviction produced repentance, repentance produced salvation, and salvation produced revival.

That is what is missing in the church today. Where are the sermons that cut? Where are the messages that drive men to the altar in tears? Where are the preachers who care more about souls than about applause?

Without conviction, there is no Pentecost power. Without conviction, there is no revival. Without conviction, the church is just a social club with religious songs.

> REVELATION 3:19 (KJV)
>
> *"As many as I love, I rebuke and chasten: be zealous therefore, and repent."*

Hear this clearly: conviction is not cruelty. It is love. When God rebukes, it is because He longs to restore. When He chastens, it is because He desires repentance. Conviction is proof of His mercy, because He loves us too much to leave us in our sin.

But when the church refuses conviction, it refuses love. When pastors silence the rebuke of the Lord, they silence the very mercy that could save souls.

The Danger of No Conviction

Without conviction, sin thrives. Without conviction, pulpits fill with flatterers and pews fill with hypocrites. Without conviction, the church looks like the world and loses all authority to call the world to Christ. Without conviction, hell fills while churches applaud.

This is the great tragedy of our age—a church without conviction cannot produce true converts. It can only produce consumers.

The Contrast of True Conviction

Every revival in history was birthed by conviction. Men and women wept under the weight of their sin. Preachers thundered holiness with tears in their eyes. Altars were stained with repentance. Whole cities trembled at the word of God.

Revival will not come through smoke machines or programs. It will come when pulpits tremble again with holy conviction. It will come when men and women are cut to the heart and cry out, "What must I do to be saved?"

The Call

It is time to restore conviction to the church. Preach the cross. Preach sin. Preach judgment. Preach holiness. Preach repentance. Preach the blood. Preach the fire of the Holy Ghost. Refuse to tickle ears. Refuse to flatter flesh. Refuse to apologize for truth.

A church without conviction is a church without Christ. Let us return before it is too late.

CHAPTER 16: A CHURCH WITHOUT CONVICTION

TRUMPET CALL

- The Spirit convicts; the church must not silence Him.
- Without conviction, there is no repentance, and without repentance, there is no salvation.
- Pastors, preach the sword of the word, not the pillows of compromise.
- Let the altars burn again with tears of repentance.

REFLECTION QUESTIONS

1. Do my sermons convict or only comfort?
2. Am I more concerned with pleasing people than with pleasing God?
3. When was the last time I wept in repentance before the Lord?
4. Do I allow the Spirit to pierce me with conviction, or do I resist Him?
5. Has my church traded truth for flattery?
6. Will I choose the offense of the cross, or the applause of men?

DECLARATION

I will not be part of a church without conviction.

I will not silence the Spirit or dull the sword of the word.

I will preach truth, even when it pierces.

I will welcome rebuke, knowing it is love.

I will weep for sin, repent of compromise, and call others to holiness.

By the Spirit's fire, I will be a voice of conviction in an age of comfort.

CHAPTER 17: The Gospel That Costs Nothing, Changes Nothing

LUKE 9:23 (KJV)

"And he said to them all, If any man will come after me, let him deny himself, and take up his cross daily, and follow me."

The call of Jesus has never changed. To follow Him is to die to self, to take up the cross daily, and to walk in obedience. This is the gospel of the kingdom—costly, confrontational, and transformational.

But in this hour, a counterfeit gospel is being preached. It promises heaven without repentance, blessing without obedience, salvation without surrender. It tells people they can have Christ without the cross, forgiveness without forsaking sin, and eternal life without a transformed life.

This is not the gospel of Jesus Christ. It is another gospel, a powerless, perverted message that comforts sinners on their way to hell.

MATTHEW 16:24–25 (KJV)

"Then said Jesus unto his disciples, If any man will come after me, let him deny himself, and take up his cross, and follow me. For whosoever will save his life shall lose it: and whosoever will lose his life for my sake shall find it."

CHAPTER 17: THE GOSPEL THAT COSTS NOTHING, CHANGES NOTHING

The true gospel demands everything. It demands your life. It demands that you surrender your rights, ambitions, and self-will, and bow to Christ as Lord. Anything less is not salvation; it is deception.

Yet pulpits today preach comfort instead of the cross. They preach "living your best life" instead of losing your life. They preach self-esteem instead of self-denial. And the fruit is clear: multitudes who wear the name of Christ but bear none of His marks.

TITUS 2:11-12 (KJV)

"For the grace of God that bringeth salvation hath appeared to all men, Teaching us that, denying ungodliness and worldly lusts, we should live soberly, righteously, and godly, in this present world."

Grace does not excuse sin; it empowers us to overcome sin. Grace is not permission to live as we please; it is power to live as He pleases. The true gospel brings transformation. It teaches us to deny ungodliness, to renounce lust, to live holy.

But the cheap gospel preached today redefines grace as tolerance. It tells us God loves us "as we are" and leaves us there. That is not grace; that is poison. Grace finds us where we are but never leaves us where it found us.

HEBREWS 12:14 (KJV)

"Follow peace with all men, and holiness, without which no man shall see the Lord."

Without holiness, no man shall see the Lord. Not one. It does not matter how many prayers were repeated, how many church services were attended, or how many times a name was written in a membership book. If there is no holiness, there is no heaven.

But a gospel without cost strips holiness away. It says, "Just believe," without repentance. It says, "Just accept Him," without surrender. It says, "Just attend church," without transformation. This false gospel has produced a church full of professors but not possessors, hearers but not doers, believers in word but not in deed.

JAMES 2:17 (KJV)

"Even so faith, if it hath not works, is dead, being alone."

Faith that does not produce obedience is not faith at all; it is dead. True faith always brings forth fruit. True salvation always produces a new life. True grace always transforms.

If the gospel you heard costs you nothing, it will change you nothing about you. And if it changes you nothing, it will save you nothing.

The Danger of a Costless Gospel

A gospel without cost produces Christians without conviction. It fills pews but empties heaven. It produces excitement without endurance, noise without power, religion without repentance. It is the gospel of Cain—sacrifice without blood, worship without obedience, offering without surrender.

The danger is eternal. Multitudes who think they are saved are not. Multitudes who think they are secure are not. They heard a half-gospel, believed a half-truth, and are living a whole lie.

The True Gospel

The true gospel is not easy, but it is glorious. It costs everything, but it gives eternal life. It crucifies the flesh, but it resurrects the spirit. It strips away sin, but it clothes us in righteousness. It calls us to die, but in dying we live.

CHAPTER 17: THE GOSPEL THAT COSTS NOTHING, CHANGES NOTHING

This is the only gospel that saves. Not the gospel of comfort, but the gospel of the cross. Not the gospel of success, but the gospel of surrender. Not the gospel of ease, but the gospel of endurance.

The Call

The time has come to preach the costly gospel again. To thunder repentance. To demand surrender. To call men to holiness. To exalt Christ as Lord, not just Savior. To declare boldly: salvation is free, but it will cost you everything.

For the gospel that costs nothing changes nothing. But the gospel of the kingdom, costly and consuming, changes everything.

TRUMPET CALL

- The gospel without cost is no gospel at all.
- Grace is not permission for sin, but power over sin.
- Without holiness, no man shall see the Lord.
- Preach the cross again—repentance, surrender, holiness, and fire.

REFLECTION QUESTIONS

1. Has my gospel been one of comfort, or of the cross?
2. Do I see grace as license or as power to live holy?
3. Am I living a transformed life, or just a church life?
4. Does my faith produce fruit, or is it dead and empty?
5. What has following Jesus cost me?
6. Would Paul, Peter, or Jesus recognize the gospel I preach and believe?

DECLARATION

I reject the cheap gospel that costs nothing and changes nothing.

I embrace the gospel of the kingdom—costly, crucifying, and glorious.

I will preach repentance, holiness, and surrender, no matter the cost.

I will not water down grace, but declare its true power to transform.

I will follow Christ with my cross, even unto death.

The gospel that saved me is the gospel that will sustain me—Christ crucified, risen, and returning.

CHAPTER 18: A Call to the New Shepherds

1 Timothy 4:12 (KJV)

"Let no man despise thy youth; but be thou an example of the believers, in word, in conversation, in charity, in spirit, in faith, in purity."

God is raising a new generation of shepherds. In an hour when many pulpits have fallen and many shepherds have forsaken their calling, the Spirit of the Lord is stirring up fresh voices—young and old—who will not bow to Baal, who will not sell out for applause, and who will not be silent when wolves approach the flock.

This is a call to you, new shepherds. You are not called to perform. You are not called to entertain. You are not called to build your brand. You are called to feed the sheep.

John 21:15–17 (KJV)

"So when they had dined, Jesus saith to Simon Peter, Simon, son of Jonas, lovest thou me more than these? He saith unto him Yea Lord; thou knowest that I love thee. He saith unto him, Feed my lambs.

He saith unto him again the second time, Simon, son of Jonas, lovest thou me? He saith unto him, Yea, Lord; Thou knowest that I love thee. He saith unto him, Feed my sheep.

TO THE SHEPHERDS

He saith unto him the third time, Simon, son of Jonas, lovest thou me? Peter was grieved because he said unto him the third time, Lovest thou me? And he said unto him, Lord, thou knowest all things; thou knowest that I love thee. Jesus saith unto him, Feed my sheep."

This is the first and final charge of every shepherd: feed His sheep. Not with opinions. Not with trends. Not with motivational speeches. But with the word of the Living God. Sheep do not live on entertainment; they live on bread. And Christ has commanded: "Feed My sheep."

A new shepherd's greatest duty is to set the table of God's word before hungry souls. If you do not feed them, they will starve. If you feed them poison, they will die. If you feed them truth, they will live.

JEREMIAH 3:15 (KJV)

"And I will give you pastors according to mine heart, which shall feed you with knowledge and understanding."

New shepherds, you must understand your true work:
- Preach the word with boldness (2 Tim 4:2). Do not scratch itching ears. Do not water down the cross. Declare "Thus saith the Lord."
- Feed the flock with truth (Jer 3:15). Do not waste their time with stories and jokes while their souls starve.
- Guard the sheep from wolves (Acts 20:29–30). False doctrine and deception will try to destroy them. You must protect them with truth and courage.
- Lead by example (1 Pet 5:2–3). You cannot take the sheep where you refuse to go. Live holy. Live humble. Live in prayer.
- Pray for the flock (Col 1:9). True shepherds weep in secret for their sheep.

CHAPTER 18: A CALL TO THE NEW SHEPHERDS

- Bind up the broken; seek the lost (Ezek 34:16). Shepherds carry the heart of Christ for the least, the weak, and the forgotten.

This is your work, not building a platform, not gaining followers, not perfecting stage presence. Your work is to watch for souls.

HEBREWS 13:17 (KJV)

"Obey them that have the rule over you, and submit yourselves: for they watch for your souls, as they that must give account."

New shepherds, the souls entrusted to you are not numbers. They are eternal. You will give an account of how you handled them.
- Did you preach truth, or did you flatter?
- Did you guard them from wolves, or did you leave the gate open?
- Did you lead them toward holiness, or toward compromise?
- Did you love them enough to wound them with truth, or did you abandon them for applause?

The flock is not yours. It is Christ's. He purchased it with His own blood (Acts 20:28). To mishandle the sheep is to insult the Shepherd. To scatter the sheep is to incur His wrath.

EZEKIEL 33:6 (KJV)

"But if the watchman see the sword come, and blow not the trumpet, and the people be not warned . . . his blood will I require at the watchman's hand."

This is the holy fear you must carry: if you do not warn, their blood will be on your hands.

TO THE SHEPHERDS

JEREMIAH 23:1–2 (KJV)

"Woe be unto the pastors that destroy and scatter the sheep of my pasture! saith the LORD."

Woe to shepherds who scatter by silence, neglect, or compromise.

JAMES 3:1 (KJV)

"My brethren, be not many masters, knowing that we shall receive the greater condemnation."

Shepherd, your judgment will be stricter. You will answer not only for your own soul, but for those you led.

Unfaithful shepherds will not only lose their pulpits; they will lose their place before the Lord. God Himself will remove them (Ezek 34:10).

1 PETER 5:4 (KJV)

"And when the chief Shepherd shall appear, ye shall receive a crown of glory that fadeth not away."

If you are faithful, your reward will not be applause on earth, but a crown in heaven. You may not be known on earth, but you will be known in eternity.

But if you are unfaithful, you will face shame before the very Chief Shepherd you claimed to serve.

This call is not easy. It will cost you your reputation. It will cost you comfort. It may even cost you your life. But Christ is worth it.
- You are not called to be popular, but faithful.
- You are not called to be successful, but holy.
- You are not called to entertain, but to intercede.

CHAPTER 18: A CALL TO THE NEW SHEPHERDS

Your work is not measured in numbers, but in souls. Heaven will not ask how many followers you had, but how many sheep you kept from wolves.

TRUMPET CALL

- Feed the sheep with truth, not fables.
- Guard the flock with courage, even if it costs you.
- Warn the wicked, lest their blood be on your hands.
- Remember: the flock is Christ's, purchased with His blood.
- Live holy, pray fervently, preach boldly, and endure faithfully.

REFLECTION QUESTIONS

1. Do I see the flock as mine, or as Christ's?
2. Am I feeding the sheep with truth or entertaining them with fables?
3. Have I been faithful to warn, or silent in fear?
4. Do I carry the fear of God, knowing I will give account for their souls?
5. Am I willing to endure hardness as a soldier of Christ?
6. Will I receive the crown of glory or the woe of judgment?

DECLARATION

I will feed the sheep entrusted to me with the word of God.

I will guard the flock, knowing they are purchased by Christ's blood.

I will not seek applause, platforms, or success, but holiness and faithfulness.

I will endure hardness as a soldier of Christ.

I will carry His heart for the broken, the weak, and the lost.

I will warn the wicked and strengthen the faithful.

By His Spirit, I will be a faithful shepherd until the Chief Shepherd returns.

CHAPTER 19: **Entertained but Not Transformed**

2 Timothy 4:3–4 (KJV)

"For the time will come when they will not endure sound doctrine; but after their own lusts shall they heap to themselves teachers, having itching ears; And they shall turn away their ears from the truth, and shall be turned unto fables."

The church today is full, but not full of power. Crowds are gathering. Programs are running. Lights are shining. Music is playing. But the altars are empty, the hearts are unchanged, and the world is still dying in its sin.

We have built services that entertain but don't convict. Worship that stirs emotions but never reaches the spirit. Sermons that inspire the flesh but never crucify it. And it is killing us.

This was prophesied. Paul said the day would come when people would no longer tolerate sound doctrine. They would demand teachers who scratch their itching ears—preachers who validate sin, bless rebellion, and replace repentance with motivational slogans. That day is not coming. That day is here.

TO THE SHEPHERDS

1 Corinthians 2:4 (KJV)

"And my speech and my preaching was not with enticing words of man's wisdom, but in demonstration of the Spirit and of power."

The early church did not win the world with eloquence, performance, or showmanship. They turned the world upside down with the raw fire of the Holy Ghost. Their sermons cut to the heart. Their prayers shook prison cells. Their witness drove demons out and healed the sick.

But today, pulpits trade fire for flash. Sermons are polished but powerless. Services are impressive but empty. Worship is loud but lifeless. We have mistaken noise for anointing and applause for revival.

Entertainment stirs the soul but leaves the spirit untouched. It produces emotion but not repentance. It fills chairs but not altars. It builds crowds but not crosses.

Hebrews 4:12 (KJV)

"For the word of God is quick, and powerful, and sharper than any twoedged sword, piercing even to the dividing asunder of soul and spirit."

The word of God was never meant to amuse. It was meant to pierce. It is not a feather that tickles; it is a sword that cuts. It divides flesh from spirit, sin from righteousness, lies from truth.

But in many pulpits, the sword has been sheathed. Pastors often avoid hard truths so no one feels offended. They preach smooth things so the crowds keep coming. And the result is a church that feels good on Sunday and lives unchanged on Monday.

CHAPTER 19: ENTERTAINED BUT NOT TRANSFORMED

A word that never wounds will never heal. A gospel that never confronts will never convert. A sermon that never pierces will never produce repentance.

REVELATION 3:1 (KJV)

"Thou hast a name that thou livest, and art dead."

The danger of entertainment-driven Christianity is that it looks alive. The buildings are packed. The music is excellent. The atmosphere is electric. People say, "This is life!" But Jesus says, "You are dead."

We have mistaken activity for anointing, busyness for brokenness, charisma for consecration. But the church with the most programs is not always the church with the most presence.

The truth is this: a church that entertains but does not transform is already under judgment. It has a name that it lives, but it is dead.

JEREMIAH 23:29 (KJV)

"Is not my word like as a fire? saith the LORD; and like a hammer that breaketh the rock in pieces?"

Real preaching is fire. It burns up sin. It breaks chains. It smashes pride. It melts hearts. It hammers rebellion until it shatters.

Real worship does not need smoke machines because it carries the cloud of glory. It does not need hype because it has holiness. It does not need a stage show because it has the presence of the living God.

Entertainment can fill a room, but only the fire of God can fill a soul.

ACTS 2:37 (KJV)

"Now when they heard this, they were pricked in their heart, and said unto Peter and to the rest of the apostles, Men and brethren, what shall we do?"

This is the mark of true preaching—hearts pricked, sin exposed, people crying out, "What must we do?" Revival does not begin with applause. It begins with tears.

The church must return to preaching the blood, the cross, repentance, judgment, mercy, holiness, and fire. Enough of tickled ears; let hearts burn again.

- Entertainment produces excitement. The cross produces repentance.
- Entertainment makes fans. The gospel makes disciples.
- Entertainment fills buildings. The Spirit fills men with boldness.
- Entertainment pleases crowds. The word pleases Christ.

Jesus did not come to entertain. He came to transform. He did not die to improve our mood. He died to save our souls.

CHAPTER 19: ENTERTAINED BUT NOT TRANSFORMED

TRUMPET CALL

- The church is not a theater; it is a temple.
- Stop feeding itching ears and start piercing hearts.
- Do not mistake applause for revival.
- Return to the word that burns, the cross that convicts, the fire that transforms.

REFLECTION QUESTIONS

1. Do I preach to stir emotions or to pierce hearts?
2. Have I substituted performance for presence in my ministry?
3. Do my sermons entertain or transform?
4. Is my church alive in Christ, or only alive in activity?
5. Am I willing to trade applause for anointing, and crowds for the cross?

DECLARATION

I will not entertain a dying world; I will confront it with truth.

I will not tickle ears; I will pierce hearts with the word of God.

I will not trade fire for flash, or power for performance.

I will preach Christ crucified, risen, and returning.

I will seek transformation, not entertainment—revival, not relevance.

I will live and minister for the approval of Christ, not the applause of men.

CHAPTER 20: **A Church Without Conviction**

JOHN 16:8 (KJV)

"And when he is come, he will reprove the world of sin, and of righteousness, and of judgment."

The mark of a Spirit-filled church is not its music, its programs, or even its crowds. The true mark is conviction. When the Holy Spirit moves, sin is exposed, hearts are pierced, and men fall to their knees, crying out for mercy.

But today, much of the church has silenced conviction. We preach comfort but not correction. We exalt grace but neglect repentance. We sing about the cross but never call people to carry it. We soothe consciences instead of stirring them. And without conviction, there can be no conversion.

HEBREWS 12:14 (KJV)

"Follow peace with all men, and holiness, without which no man shall see the Lord."

Holiness has become optional in the modern pulpit. Preachers avoid calling sin by its name for fear of losing members, offerings, or online followers. The cry for holiness has been replaced with motivational speeches. The call to repentance has been exchanged for affirmations of self.

CHAPTER 20: A CHURCH WITHOUT CONVICTION

But a church without conviction is not a church at all—it is a social club wearing religious clothes. It may have energy, lights, and music, but it has no fire. It may fill seats, but it does not fill altars. It may inspire, but it does not transform.

Conviction is not cruelty—it is mercy. It is the scalpel of the Spirit that cuts in order to heal. It is the hammer that breaks pride so humility can be born. It is the light that exposes sin so grace can cover it.

Revelation 3:19 (KJV)

"As many as I love, I rebuke and chasten: be zealous therefore, and repent."

God convicts because He loves. A father who never corrects his children does not love them—he abandons them. And a preacher who never convicts his people does not love them—he abandons their souls to hell.

Amos 8:11 (KJV)

"Behold, the days come, saith the Lord GOD, that I will send a famine in the land, not a famine of bread, nor a thirst for water, but of hearing the words of the LORD."

We are living in that famine. Sermons are everywhere, but truth is rare. Words are many, but conviction is absent. The famine is not one of availability; it is one of courage.

The cost of this silence is eternal. Souls walk into church bound by sin and leave bound still. People clap for sermons that never confront their chains. Altars remain dry, and revival tarries. And God weeps.

2 Timothy 3:5 (KJV)

"Having a form of godliness, but denying the power thereof: from such turn away."

The church does not need more polish; it needs more power. And power only comes when the word is preached without compromise. When sin is called sin. When holiness is lifted high. When the fear of the Lord returns to the pulpit.

The prophets of old were not applauded; they were hated, imprisoned, stoned, and rejected. But their words carried fire. And that fire turned hearts back to God. Where are the watchmen today who will dare to preach like Jeremiah, like Amos, like John the baptist?

We need preachers who would rather offend men than offend God. We need pulpits that tremble again under the weight of truth.

Acts 2:37 (KJV)

"Now when they heard this, they were pricked in their heart, and said unto Peter and to the rest of the apostles, Men and brethren, what shall we do?"

This is the fruit of true preaching—men cut to the heart. Conviction is the fire that melts the sinner into repentance. It is the voice that drives the prodigal back home. It is the holy ache that makes men weep at the altar until grace floods their souls.

Conviction produces holiness. Conviction produces repentance. Conviction produces revival. Without it, all we have is noise. With it, the world is turned upside down.

CHAPTER 20: A CHURCH WITHOUT CONVICTION

TRUMPET CALL

- Without conviction, there is no conversion.
- Shepherds, preach the word, even when it offends.
- Do not silence the Spirit. Let Him pierce, let Him expose, let Him heal.
- The church must return to the altar of repentance, not the stage of entertainment.
- Revival will not come through comfort, but through conviction.

REFLECTION QUESTIONS

1. Do I welcome conviction in my life, or resist it?
2. Has my church substituted comfort for correction?
3. Do I preach what people want to hear, or what God commands me to speak?
4. Am I living in holiness, or excusing sin in the name of grace?
5. Would my ministry survive without the approval of men?
6. When was the last time I wept under the weight of God's conviction?

DECLARATION

I will not run from conviction; I will embrace it.

I will not silence the Spirit's voice; I will yield to it.

I will not preach comfort when God demands correction.

I will not trade holiness for popularity, or repentance for applause.

I will walk in holiness and preach with fire, no matter the cost.

By His Spirit, I will be a voice of conviction in an age of compromise.

CHAPTER 21: Shepherds, Wake the Sleeping Flock

ROMANS 13:11 (KJV)

"And that, knowing the time, that now it is high time to awake out of sleep: for now is our salvation nearer than when we believed."

The flock is asleep. Their eyes are heavy with comfort, their ears dulled by entertainment, their hearts numbed by compromise. They slumber in the very hour when vigilance is needed most. The bridegroom is at the door, yet the lamps of many sit dark and cold.

And where are the shepherds? Many are asleep themselves. Some are distracted by programs, others by platforms, and too many by the praise of men. Yet God did not call His shepherds to soothe sheep into slumber; He called them to wake the flock.

MATTHEW 25:5-6 (KJV)

"While the bridegroom tarried, they all slumbered and slept. And at midnight there was a cry made, Behold, the bridegroom cometh; go ye out to meet him."

This is the state of much of the modern church. The wise and foolish alike have grown drowsy. The oil runs low. The fire flickers. The cry has gone out, yet only a few are rising to trim their lamps.

CHAPTER 21: SHEPHERDS, WAKE THE SLEEPING FLOCK

The sleeping flock is not without hope, but they cannot wake themselves. Someone must cry out, "The bridegroom is coming!" Someone must shake them from apathy, call them to repentance, and prepare them for His appearing. That someone is the shepherd.

> EZEKIEL 33:6 (KJV)
>
> *"But if the watchman see the sword come, and blow not the trumpet, and the people be not warned; if the sword come, and take any person from among them, he is taken away in his iniquity; but his blood will I require at the watchman's hand."*

The shepherd is a watchman. His eyes are meant to scan the horizon for danger, his voice to sound the trumpet when wolves approach. But what happens when the watchman sleeps? When the shepherd refuses to sound the alarm? The sheep remain in danger, and God holds the shepherd accountable.

Shepherd, this is your calling: to wake the flock, not to rock them back to sleep with soothing words. Your sermons are not meant to entertain; they are meant to rattle the soul awake. Your worship sets are not meant to create a mood; they are designed to ignite a holy fire. Your leadership is not about maintaining comfort; it is about preparing warriors.

If you fail, their blood is on your hands.

> JOEL 2:1 (KJV)
>
> *"Blow ye the trumpet in Zion, and sound an alarm in my holy mountain: let all the inhabitants of the land tremble: for the day of the LORD cometh, for it is nigh at hand."*

The trumpet is not optional; it is commanded. The day of the Lord is near. The judgment of God is real. Yet many pulpits stay silent. They speak of blessings but never of sin. They declare prosperity

TO THE SHEPHERDS

but never repentance. They soothe consciences when they should be piercing them.

Shepherds who will not blow the trumpet create churches unprepared for battle. Sheep that are never warned remain blind to the wolf. Silence is not kindness; it is cruelty.

> ACTS 20:26–27 (KJV)
>
> *"Wherefore I take you to record this day, that I am pure from the blood of all men. For I have not shunned to declare unto you all the counsel of God."*

Paul declared himself innocent of men's blood because he did not shrink back from preaching the full counsel of God. But shepherds who refuse to preach truth—who dodge holiness, avoid hell, and silence the Spirit—will stand guilty before the throne.

The cost of neglect is eternal. Sheep led by silent shepherds will face judgment unprepared. And God will say to those leaders, "Their blood I require at your hands."

The shepherd is not a performer. He is not a celebrity. He is not a CEO. He is a watchman, a guardian, a trumpet. His task is not to soothe, but to stir. Not to entertain, but to awaken. Not to pacify, but to prepare.

When the shepherd cries aloud, sheep arise. When the shepherd warns, lamps are trimmed. When the shepherd preaches repentance, altars are filled. A true shepherd wakes the flock, even if they resent him for it. Better a flock offended into holiness than one soothed into hell.

> REVELATION 3:2 (KJV)
>
> *"Be watchful, and strengthen the things which remain, that are ready to die: for I have not found thy works perfect before God."*

CHAPTER 21: SHEPHERDS, WAKE THE SLEEPING FLOCK

This is the cry of God to His shepherds: Be watchful. Strengthen what remains. Wake the flock before it dies.

The church cannot afford sleeping leaders. The trumpet must sound. The flock must be stirred. The bride must be readied. Shepherds, wake the sheep! Do not whisper peace when the sword is at the gate. Do not preach comfort when judgment is at hand. Do not soothe when God says shout.

The hour is late. The bridegroom is coming. Shepherds, wake the flock.

TRUMPET CALL

- Shepherds, the flock is asleep; wake them with truth.
- Do not rock them into slumber with soothing sermons.
- Blow the trumpet, sound the alarm, pierce the silence.
- Better to offend sheep into holiness than to soothe them into hell.
- The bridegroom is coming. Wake the flock before it is too late.

REFLECTION QUESTIONS

1. Do I preach in a way that wakes people up, or lulls them to sleep?
2. Have I silenced the trumpet of warning in fear of losing approval?
3. Do I carry the burden of a watchman, or the comfort of an entertainer?
4. Have I declared the whole counsel of God, or only the parts that please?
5. Am I willing to bear reproach for waking the flock, even if they resent me?

DECLARATION

I will not sleep while the flock slumbers.

I will not silence the trumpet when danger is at the gate.

I will not preach peace when God says, "Repent."

I will wake the sheep entrusted to me with truth, holiness, and fire.

By His Spirit, I will sound the alarm until the bride is ready, and the bridegroom comes again.

CHAPTER 22: When the Pulpit Lost Its Tears

JEREMIAH 9:1 (KJV)

"Oh that my head were waters, and mine eyes a fountain of tears, that I might weep day and night for the slain of the daughter of my people!"

ACTS 20:31 (KJV)

"Therefore watch, and remember, that by the space of three years I ceased not to warn every one night and day with tears."

JOEL 2:17 (KJV)

"Let the priests, the ministers of the LORD, weep between the porch and the altar, and let them say, Spare thy people, O LORD."

The Tragedy of a Dry Pulpit

The pulpit was never meant to be a platform for performance. It was meant to be an altar, a place where fire fell and where the word of God burned through men who had been broken in His presence.

Yet today, many pulpits are dry. They echo with clever words but lack weight. They stir emotions but not repentance. They produce applause but not transformation.

Where are the tears? Where is the travail? Where is the shepherd who weeps over the flock like Paul, who warned day and night with tears? Where is the priest who collapses between the porch and the altar, crying out for mercy? Where is the pastor who cannot sleep because the sheep are wandering, who carries the burden of the Lord in his bones until he groans in prayer?

A pulpit without tears is a pulpit without power.

The Biblical Pattern of Weeping Shepherds

From Genesis to Revelation, God's true leaders were men and women of tears. Jeremiah was called "the weeping prophet." Paul confessed that he warned with tears. David's psalms are soaked with weeping. Even Jesus Himself, the Shepherd of our souls, wept over Jerusalem and groaned at Lazarus' tomb.

Tears are not weakness. Tears are the overflow of a burden too heavy to contain. Tears are evidence of a heart aligned with God's own grief. Tears reveal that the shepherd is not speaking from intellect alone, but from a broken spirit that has touched the heart of heaven.

Paul didn't build churches through marketing. He birthed them through tears. Jeremiah didn't carry revival through strategies. He carried it through weeping. Jesus didn't win souls by impressing crowds. He gave His blood and His tears.

If our Savior wept, what excuse do shepherds have for preaching with dry eyes?

CHAPTER 22: WHEN THE PULPIT LOST ITS TEARS

The Call to Weep Again

Shepherd, you cannot lead with a dry heart. You cannot preach with a calloused spirit. You cannot warn without weeping. It is time to fall on your face again until tears flow. It is time to let God break your heart for the lost, for the backslidden, for the deceived, for the church that is asleep.

When was the last time you wept in the secret place, not because of personal pain, but because of God's burden for souls? When was the last time you cried out at the altar until your voice cracked, begging the Lord to spare His people? When was the last time the reality of hell broke you?

Shepherds, the sheep are straying. Wolves are devouring. The flock is bleeding. If you are not weeping, then you are sleeping.

The Consequence of Dryness

A dry pulpit produces a dry church. A pastor without tears raises a people without repentance. Sermons without travail create congregations without transformation.

We live in a generation that claps, dances, and laughs at church, but rarely trembles, repents, or weeps. Why? Because the shepherds have lost their tears.

Where the pulpit has no burden, the altar has no fire. Where the preacher feels no grief, the people feel no conviction. Where the leaders have no tears, the flock has no revival.

If you preach without weeping, you may gather crowds, but you will not gather disciples. You may stir emotions, but you will not pierce hearts. You may entertain, but you will not transform.

The Fire of Brokenness

Revival does not begin with volume. It begins with tears. It does not begin with lights and music. It begins with brokenness. It does not begin with strategy. It begins with travail.

The prophets understood this. The apostles lived this. Jesus Himself modeled this. Shepherds, you must return to this. A shepherd with tears is dangerous to the kingdom of darkness. A shepherd broken before God cannot be bought, silenced, or swayed. His tears become his testimony, his groaning becomes his sermon, his brokenness becomes his authority.

Shepherd, let the fire of brokenness consume you. Pray until you weep. Preach until you groan. Weep until the heavens open and the Spirit falls again.

The Call to the Shepherds

This is not a suggestion; it is a command. Joel didn't say, "Ministers, try to weep." He said, "Let the priests weep between the porch and the altar." Shepherd, if you are not weeping, you are disobeying. If you are not broken, you are not ready. If you are not burdened, you are not prepared.

God is calling His shepherds back to the altar, not to play, not to perform, but to weep. Only then will the flock awaken. Only then will revival break out. Only then will the fire fall again.

CHAPTER 22: WHEN THE PULPIT LOST ITS TEARS

TRUMPET CALL

- Shepherd, a pulpit without tears is powerless.
- Return to the altar. Let the burden of the Lord break you.
- Do not preach with a dry heart; let your eyes be fountains again.
- Revival begins where shepherds weep.

REFLECTION QUESTIONS

1. Do I preach with a burden, or with empty words?
2. When was the last time tears stained my Bible or my altar?
3. Have I grown comfortable, hardened, or casual in the pulpit?
4. Am I warning with tears, like Paul, or entertaining with jokes?
5. Would my people say I carry God's burden, or only my own ambitions?

DECLARATION

I refuse to preach with dry eyes.

I refuse to stand in a pulpit without a burden.

I will weep between the porch and the altar until the fire falls again.

I will warn with tears, pray with tears, and preach with tears.

I will let the grief of God break me, so His Spirit can burn through me.

I am not a performer. I am a watchman.

And I will not lose my tears until I see His glory return to His church.

CHAPTER 23: Scattered by Silence, Wounded by Words

JEREMIAH 23:1-2 (KJV)

"Woe be unto the pastors that destroy and scatter the sheep of my pasture! saith the LORD. Therefore thus saith the LORD God of Israel against the pastors that feed my people; Ye have scattered my flock, and driven them away, and have not visited them: behold, I will visit upon you the evil of your doings, saith the LORD."

EZEKIEL 34:4 (KJV)

"The diseased have ye not strengthened, neither have ye healed that which was sick, neither have ye bound up that which was broken, neither have ye brought again that which was driven away, neither have ye sought that which was lost; but with force and with cruelty have ye ruled them."

Scattered by Silence

The sheep are hungry. They gather week after week, searching for bread from heaven, water from the Spirit, and the voice of God through His word. Yet many pulpits offer stones instead of bread.

CHAPTER 23: SCATTERED BY SILENCE, WOUNDED BY WORDS

Clever phrases instead of truth. Opinions instead of Scripture. Comfort instead of conviction.

And what happens when sheep are not fed? They scatter. Not because they hate God. Not because they despise His word. But because the shepherd gave them nothing that could sustain them.

Amos prophesied of a famine, not of bread, but of hearing the word of the Lord (Amos 8:11). That famine is here. Churches are full of programs but empty of presence. Sermons are long on stories but short on Scripture. The fire has gone out of the altar, and silence reigns where a trumpet should be blasting.

When the shepherd loses his fire, the sheep lose their way.

Wounded by Words

If silence starves the flock, cruelty scatters it. Some sheep don't leave because they were unfed; they leave because they were wounded by the very man called to heal them.

How many times have pastors used their pulpits as platforms for their own opinions? How many have lashed out in anger, shamed people publicly, or condemned individuals to hell with their own words? These are not the ways of Christ.

Jesus wept over the lost. He ate with sinners. He lifted the broken. He called the weary to rest. But some shepherds today heap shame instead of hope, condemnation instead of correction, ridicule instead of restoration.

The sheep come seeking the Shepherd's heart and instead receive a whip of man's pride. And so they leave. Not because they despise Christ, but because they could not find Him in the voice of their pastor.

The Heart of the True Shepherd

Jesus said, "I am the good shepherd: the good shepherd giveth his life for the sheep" (John 10:11). A true shepherd lays himself down for the flock. He binds up the broken, strengthens the weak, restores the fallen, and feeds the hungry.

A shepherd's words should cut when they must, but never crush. They should confront sin, but always point to grace. They should warn of hell, but never without pointing to the hope of the cross.

Paul told the Ephesians that he warned them "with tears" (Acts 20:31). Where are the tears in the pulpits today? Where is the grief over sin, mingled with the mercy of Christ? Where is the balance of truth and love, conviction and compassion?

The sheep are not meant to be scattered by their shepherd's silence, nor destroyed by his severity. They are meant to be gathered, healed, fed, and prepared for the coming of the Lord.

God's Indictment

Jeremiah 23 and Ezek 34 thunder with God's judgment against shepherds who scatter His flock. He does not take lightly the wounds inflicted by careless words or the neglect caused by empty sermons.

God says plainly: "Woe to the shepherds. If you silence the trumpet, their blood is on your hands. If you scatter with cruelty, their blood is on your hands. If you replace My word with your own voice, their blood is on your hands."

Shepherd, this is holy ground. You are not free to preach yourself. You are not free to vent your anger. You are not free to silence the cross. You are called to feed the sheep or step aside.

The Call to Feed Again

The scattered flock must be regathered. The wounded sheep must be healed. The famished must be fed. And that begins not with strategy, but with repentance.

Shepherd, return to the word. Preach the Scriptures with fire and fear of the Lord. Tear down your opinions and exalt Christ alone. Bind up the broken instead of breaking them further. Weep with the wounded instead of wounding them deeper. Strengthen the weak rather than mocking their struggles.

Let the altar burn again. Let the trumpet sound again. Let the tears flow again.

Because if the sheep cannot find Christ in the church, where shall they go?

TRUMPET CALL

- Shepherds, your silence starves the flock.
- Your cruelty wounds the sheep you were called to heal.
- Return to the word. Return to the altar. Return to the Shepherd's heart.
- Woe to the shepherds who scatter, but blessings to those who gather, feed, and restore.

REFLECTION QUESTIONS

1. Am I feeding the flock with God's word, or starving them with my silence?
2. Have my words ever wounded sheep more than they healed them?
3. Do I use the pulpit for Christ's message, or my own opinions?
4. Would the sheep say I point them to Jesus, or push them away from Him?
5. When I preach holiness, do I also preach hope?

DECLARATION

I will not scatter by silence.

I will not wound by cruelty.

I will not use the pulpit for my own voice, but for the voice of Christ.

I will feed the flock with His word, bind up the broken with His mercy, and warn with His truth.

I will carry the Shepherd's heart, full of fire, yet full of love.

By His Spirit, I will gather, not scatter; heal, not wound; and build up the sheep until the Chief Shepherd returns.

CHAPTER 24: The Weight and Wonder of the Call

1 Peter 5:2-4 (KJV)

"Feed the flock of God which is among you, taking the oversight thereof, not by constraint, but willingly; not for filthy lucre, but of a ready mind; Neither as being lords over God's heritage, but being examples to the flock. And when the chief Shepherd shall appear, ye shall receive a crown of glory that fadeth not away."

The Sacred Trust of the Flock

The call to shepherd is unlike any other call on earth. It is not a career path, a personal ambition, or a way to make a name for yourself. It is a sacred trust given by the Lord Himself. He has entrusted you not with money, not with buildings, not with influence—but with His flock. His people. His bride.

When Jesus restored Peter after his denial, He did not ask him about strategy, charisma, or success. He asked one question: "Lovest thou me?" And when Peter affirmed his love, Jesus answered with one command: "Feed my sheep" (John 21:17).

This is the core of the shepherd's task: to feed. To nourish. To guide. To tend the flock of God with His word and His presence. A true shepherd does not treat the people as his audience, his customers, or his fan base; they are God's sheep, bought with the blood of Christ.

Ezekiel thundered God's indictment against unfaithful shepherds: "Woe be to the shepherds of Israel that do feed themselves! should not the shepherds feed the flocks?" (Ezek 34:2). The Lord accused them of neglect, of cruelty, of scattering the sheep. And He declared that He Himself would come to rescue His flock from their hands.

Shepherd, the people do not belong to you. They belong to Him. You are not the owner; you are the steward. You are not the Savior; you are the servant. You are not the King; you are the undershepherd, accountable to the Chief Shepherd.

This calling should make you tremble. To feed God's flock is to handle eternal souls. To preach is to carry the eternal word of God into hearts that will never die. To lead is to influence destinies that stretch into forever.

A Holy Burden That Breaks You

James warns us: "My brethren, be not many masters, knowing that we shall receive the greater condemnation" (Jas 3:1). Teachers, preachers, shepherds will face stricter judgment. Why? Because you influence many. Because your words can either guide to truth or lead to destruction.

Hebrews 13:17 declares: "Obey them that have the rule over you, and submit yourselves: for they watch for your souls, as they that must give account." Shepherd, you will give an account before God Himself for how you watched, how you fed, how you guided His sheep.

This is not a light responsibility. This is not a casual role. The shepherd's calling is a holy burden, and that burden is meant to break you. If you step into the pulpit and never tremble, you have lost

CHAPTER 24: THE WEIGHT AND WONDER OF THE CALL

your fear of God. If you preach without weeping over souls, you have lost His heart.

The weight of the call is not meant to crush you into despair, but to crush your pride. It is meant to strip away self-reliance and drive you to the feet of Jesus. If you carry it in your own strength, you will fall. But if you bow low, if you stay on your knees, you will find His strength made perfect in your weakness.

Vessels of Clay, Treasure Within

Paul writes: "But we have this treasure in earthen vessels, that the excellency of the power may be of God, and not of us" (2 Cor 4:7).

You are not called because you are strong. You are called because He is strong in you. God delights in using weak vessels, cracked jars, ordinary men, so that the glory is all His.

Think of Moses, stammering at the burning bush, begging God to send someone else. Think of Jeremiah, crying out, "I am a child!" Think of Gideon, hiding in fear, declaring, "My family is poor . . . and I am the least in my father's house." Think of Peter, swearing he would never deny Christ, only to fall three times before a servant girl's question.

Yet these were the ones God used. Not because they were mighty, but because they surrendered. Moses became the deliverer. Jeremiah became the weeping prophet whose words still burn today. Gideon became a judge who delivered Israel with only three hundred men. Peter became the rock who preached the first sermon of the gospel at Pentecost.

Your weakness is not your disqualification. It is your qualification for grace. God is not looking for flawless men. He is looking for surrendered men. Men who know they are clay, but who carry a treasure not their own.

Shepherd, stop despising your weakness. Stop hiding your scars. Stop pretending to be more than you are. Let the treasure of Christ shine through your cracks. Let His strength be seen in your frailty. The sheep need Jesus, not you. And He delights to show Himself strong through broken vessels.

The Wonder of Being Chosen

Never lose the wonder of this call. Out of all the men in the world, God chose you to shepherd His flock. Not because you were the best, the smartest, or the most gifted, but because He willed it. Because He placed His hand upon you. Because His grace was sufficient.

Paul marveled at this, calling himself "the chief of sinners," yet entrusted with the gospel (1 Tim 1:15–16). He said, "Woe is unto me, if I preach not the gospel!" (1 Cor 9:16). He lived in awe of the privilege of proclaiming Christ.

When you stand in the pulpit, heaven leans in. Angels listen. Demons tremble. Eternity watches. Souls hang in the balance. Never let routine steal this awe. Never let pride dull this wonder. If preaching has become common to you, go back to the altar. If shepherding has become a job, go back to your first love.

The pulpit is not a stage. It is an altar. It is not a platform for your opinions. It is a place where heaven and earth meet, where Christ is exalted, where the word goes forth like fire and hammer, breaking rock in pieces.

Shepherd, remember the wonder. Remember that God chose you, not to build your kingdom, but to serve His.

Strength in Weakness

Paul himself bore a thorn in the flesh. He begged God to take it away, but the Lord answered: "My grace is sufficient for thee:

for my strength is made perfect in weakness" (2 Cor 12:9). Paul learned to glory in his infirmities, because through them Christ's power rested on him.

Moses had no eloquence, yet God put His words in his mouth. Jeremiah was too young, yet God put fire in his bones. Gideon was too weak, yet God clothed him with His Spirit. Peter was too unstable, yet God made him a pillar.

Do you see? Weakness is not an obstacle. It is the very place where His strength is revealed. Brokenness is not your end. It is your beginning.

A shepherd who pretends to be strong will fail. A shepherd who confesses his weakness will find strength from heaven. God does not need your polish, your wit, your charisma. He requires your surrender. He requires your tears. He requires your humility.

The Coming Reward

This burden is heavy, but it will not last forever. One day, the Chief Shepherd will appear, and then the reward will come.

Peter promised a "crown of glory that fadeth not away" (1 Pet 5:4). Paul spoke of the *crown of righteousness* laid up for those who love His appearing (2 Tim 4:8). James wrote of the *crown of life* promised to those who endure temptation (Jas 1:12). Paul also spoke of the *incorruptible crown* for those who run the race faithfully (1 Cor 9:25).

These are not crowns of man's applause. They are not medals for earthly success. They are eternal rewards given by Christ Himself.

On that day, shepherd, the Chief Shepherd will look you in the eye. Not your congregation. Not your peers. Not the world. Jesus Himself. And He will ask: Did you feed My sheep? Did you preach My word? Did you carry My heart? Did you endure until the end?

No applause here can compare to His "Well done, thou good and faithful servant." No recognition here can rival the glory of receiving a crown from His hand.

The Crown and the Cross

But remember this: there is no crown without the cross. Jesus said, "If any man will come after me, let him deny himself, and take up his cross daily, and follow me" (Luke 9:23).

Shepherd, you must bleed before you reign. You must suffer before you glory. You must carry the cross before you wear the crown.

This call is not about comfort. It is not about crowds. It is not about applause. It is about sacrifice. It is about dying daily. It is about laying down your life as Christ laid down His.

The road is narrow. The way is costly. The pain is real. But the glory is eternal.

The Balance of Fear and Joy

So hold both truths close:
- The fear of the Lord—for you will give an account.
- The joy of the Lord—for you are His co-laborer.

The fear keeps you trembling. The joy keeps you rejoicing. The fear keeps you humble. The joy keeps you strong.

Shepherd, embrace the weight and the wonder. Tremble, but also rejoice. Weep, but also sing. Bow low, but also look high. For the day is coming when the Chief Shepherd Himself will appear, and the faithful will shine like the stars forever.

CHAPTER 24: THE WEIGHT AND WONDER OF THE CALL

TRUMPET CALL

- Shepherd, the call you carry is sacred and eternal.
- Tremble under the weight, but rejoice in the wonder.
- Feed the flock. Bind the broken. Guard the sheep.
- Never forget: there is no crown without the cross, but the crown is coming.

REFLECTION QUESTIONS

1. Do I treat this call as common, or do I tremble under its weight?
2. Have I lost the wonder of being chosen to shepherd God's flock?
3. Am I feeding His sheep with His word, or with my opinions?
4. Do I lean on my strength, or His Spirit?
5. Am I preparing for man's applause, or for Christ's crown?

DECLARATION

I embrace the weight and wonder of this call.

I will not despise the burden, for it drives me to Christ.

I will not lose the awe, for it is a privilege to serve His bride.

I will preach His word, not mine; feed His sheep, not myself; seek His glory, not my own.

Though I am clay, I carry treasure.

Though I am weak, His strength is my portion.

I will carry the cross faithfully until the Chief Shepherd returns with my crown.

CHAPTER 25: **Strength for the Weary Shepherd**

ISAIAH 40:29–31 (KJV)

"He giveth power to the faint; and to them that have no might he increaseth strength. Even the youths shall faint and be weary, and the young men shall utterly fall: But they that wait upon the LORD shall renew their strength; they shall mount up with wings as eagles; they shall run, and not be weary; and they shall walk, and not faint."

The Weariness Few Admit

Shepherd, if you've ever dragged yourself into the pulpit empty, you are not alone. If you've prayed and felt nothing, preached and seen no response, or poured yourself out only to face criticism, you are not alone. Elijah, fresh from calling down fire on Mount Carmel, collapsed under a juniper tree and begged God to take his life (1 Kgs 19:4). Jeremiah said he would not speak the word anymore, but confessed that it burned like fire in his bones (Jer 20:9). Paul was "pressed out of measure, above strength, insomuch that [he] despaired even of life" (2 Cor 1:8).

Weariness is not unique to you. It is the silent plague of ministry. The pulpit can be a place of power, but also a place of pressure. Shepherding is not only about preaching—it is about carrying souls, praying through nights, bearing burdens unseen by the sheep. And yes, shepherd, it will wear you down.

But here's the truth: God has not called you to quit when you're weary. He has called you to wait on Him and be renewed.

When Shepherds Quit

The tragedy of our generation is not only wolves scattering sheep. It is shepherds laying down their staff in discouragement. Many have walked away from pulpits, not because they were disqualified by sin, but because they were drained by weariness.

But hear me: a weary shepherd is still accountable. The flock doesn't stop needing feeding because you feel tired. Souls don't stop going to hell because you've lost your spark. The kingdom doesn't pause because you're discouraged. Shepherd, your weariness cannot excuse your silence.

Jesus Himself grew weary (John 4:6). He slept in storms. He cried in Gethsemane. He bled on Calvary. Yet He did not quit. And if the Son of God endured until the end, how much more must we, by His Spirit, finish our course?

God's Answer to Weariness

God never rebuked Elijah for being tired. He fed him. He gave him rest. Then He recommissioned him: "Go, return on thy way" (1 Kgs 19:15). Elijah didn't get to stay under the juniper tree. Neither do you.

Jesus said, "Come unto me, all ye that labour and are heavy laden, and I will give you rest" (Matt 11:28). This is not the rest of resignation; it is the rest of renewal. He doesn't invite shepherds to quit, but to be filled again in His presence.

Isaiah declares, "They that wait upon the LORD shall renew their strength" (Isa 40:31). To wait is not passive. It is not sitting back with arms folded. It is to seek, to pray, to linger at the altar until heaven breathes again.

Shepherd, your strength will not come from self-help books or motivational podcasts. It will not come from vacations alone, or bigger crowds, or compliments from men. It comes only from waiting on the Lord.

The Danger of Ministering Empty

The most dangerous thing a shepherd can do is minister without oil. Samson rose to fight the Philistines, and he "wist not that the LORD was departed from him" (Judg 16:20). Many pulpits today thunder with sermons, but heaven is silent, because the shepherd is running on fumes.

When you preach empty, you risk producing empty disciples. When you shepherd weary but refuse renewal, you feed sheep stale bread. When your heart is dry, the flock feels it.

Better to cancel a service and fall on your face before God than to stand in a pulpit without His anointing. Better to admit your need than to pretend you are fine. The sheep don't need your polish; they need His presence.

Lift Up Your Eyes Again

The enemy loves to use weariness to distort your vision. Elijah thought he was the only prophet left. But God told him, "I have reserved . . . seven thousand in Israel, all the knees which have not bowed unto Baal" (1 Kgs 19:18).

Shepherd, you are not alone. You are not the only one still standing. You are part of a remnant. But you must lift up your eyes. Stop counting empty seats. Stop replaying harsh words. Stop magnifying wolves. Look to the harvest. Look to the cross. Look to the soon-coming Christ.

Jesus told His disciples: "Lift up your eyes, and look on the fields; for they are white already to harvest" (John 4:35). Weariness looks inward; faith looks upward. Stop staring at your weakness. Fix your eyes on His strength.

The Call to Finish

Paul, scarred by beatings, shipwrecked, betrayed, imprisoned, still declared: "I have fought a good fight, I have finished my course, I have kept the faith" (2 Tim 4:7). That is the call. Not to quit. Not to coast. To finish.

Shepherd, you don't need to finish big; you need to finish faithful. You don't need the applause of men; you need the crown of the Chief Shepherd. You don't need to trend online; you need to endure to the end.

The sheep need you to finish. Heaven is watching. Christ is waiting. Do not stop now.

TRUMPET CALL

- Shepherd, your weariness is not a license to quit; it is a summons to the altar.
- Do not resign under the juniper tree. Rise and return to the wall.
- The sheep still need feeding. The flock still needs guarding. The trumpet still needs sounding.
- Wait on the Lord, and He will renew your strength. Finish your course.

REFLECTION QUESTIONS

1. Where have I allowed weariness to silence my voice?
2. Have I mistaken exhaustion for permission to quit?
3. Am I feeding the flock out of the overflow of His Spirit, or out of my own strength?
4. When was the last time I waited on the Lord until His fire burned again?
5. Do I measure success by applause or by faithfulness to finish?

DECLARATION

I will not quit.

Though I grow weary, I will wait upon the Lord and be renewed.

I will not surrender to discouragement or defeat.

I will lift up my eyes and see the harvest before me.

By His strength, I will finish the race, keep the faith, and receive the crown of righteousness when my Chief Shepherd appears.

CHAPTER 26: **Guarding the Flock in the Last Days**

Acts 20:28–31 (KJV)

"Take heed therefore unto yourselves, and to all the flock, over the which the Holy Ghost hath made you overseers, to feed the church of God, which he hath purchased with his own blood. For I know this, that after my departing shall grievous wolves enter in among you, not sparing the flock. Also of your own selves shall men arise, speaking perverse things, to draw away disciples after them. Therefore watch, and remember, that by the space of three years I ceased not to warn every one night and day with tears."

The Charge to Guard

Shepherd, you are not only called to feed; you are called to guard. You are not only a preacher; you are a protector. The sheep are precious, purchased with the blood of Christ, and entrusted to your care. But in these last days, wolves are multiplying. They are bold, cunning, and relentless.

Paul wept as he warned the Ephesian elders that wolves would come, not sparing the flock. He said some would even rise up from within the church, twisting the truth for their own gain. He did not speak these words casually. He warned with tears.

The charge is clear: Watch. Guard. Protect. Sound the alarm.

Wolves in Sheep's Clothing

Jesus Himself warned: "Beware of false prophets, which come to you in sheep's clothing, but inwardly they are ravening wolves" (Matt 7:15). Wolves rarely come with snarls and blood on their fangs. They come dressed like sheep. They talk like shepherds. They quote Scripture like Satan did in the wilderness.

Shepherd, if you do not discern, your flock will be devoured. If you refuse to warn, your silence becomes complicity. Too many pulpits are silent while wolves feast. Too many shepherds refuse to name sin, refuse to expose false doctrine, refuse to confront deception. The result? Sheep are scattered, confused, and consumed.

The Danger of Neglect

Ezekiel 33 declares that the watchman who sees the sword coming and does not blow the trumpet will be held accountable for the blood of the people. Shepherd, if you see deception, if you see compromise, if you see sin creeping into your flock and you do not warn them, their blood is on your hands.

Many pastors want the applause of their people more than the safety of their souls. They want to be liked more than to be faithful. They want to grow crowds more than guard sheep. But on the day of judgment, God will not ask you how many followers you had. He will ask: "Did you guard My flock?"

Guarding Against Deception

We are living in the age of deception. Jesus said that in the last days, false Christs and false prophets would arise and, if possible, deceive even the elect (Matt 24:24).

CHAPTER 26: GUARDING THE FLOCK IN THE LAST DAYS

The Internet is full of false teachers, TikTok prophets, YouTube apostles, and Instagram pastors. Smooth words, flashy lights, and polished branding—but no cross, no holiness, no repentance. Shepherd, if you do not equip your people to discern, they will be carried away.

Guard them by teaching the word in its fullness. Guard them by warning them against lies. Guard them by pointing them to the cross, to the blood, to holiness, to the fear of the Lord. Sheep trained on truth will recognize a wolf's growl no matter the disguise.

Guarding Against Sin in the Camp

Wolves are not only outside; sometimes they sit in the pews, lead worship, or even stand behind pulpits. Paul told the Corinthians to put out the man living in sin so the whole body would not be leavened (1 Cor 5:6-7). Shepherd, if you tolerate sin in the flock, you weaken the whole body.

Holiness guards the camp. Discipline protects the sheep. Love does not ignore rebellion; love confronts it. Shepherd, if you refuse to deal with sin because you fear losing people, you are not guarding the flock; you are feeding them to destruction.

The Shepherd's Weapons

You are not helpless. You have been given weapons.
- The word of God—sharper than any two-edged sword, cutting through lies and deception.
- The Spirit of God—giving discernment, wisdom, and boldness.
- Prayer—building a hedge around your people, tearing down strongholds.
- The blood of Christ—covering the flock, rebuking the devourer.

Use them. Do not preach psychology when the wolf attacks. Do not hand out self-help slogans when deception comes. Preach the word. Pray with fire. Plead the blood. Stand in the Spirit.

The Shepherd's Courage

Guarding the flock requires courage. You will be hated for exposing wolves. You will be accused of being judgmental, divisive, and unloving. But it is better to be hated for protecting the sheep than loved while they are devoured.

Paul told Timothy: "Preach the word; be instant in season, out of season; reprove, rebuke, exhort with all longsuffering and doctrine" (2 Tim 4:2). Shepherd, your job is not to entertain, but to equip. Not to soothe, but to safeguard. Not to build crowds, but to guard souls.

The Chief Shepherd is watching. The angels are recording. The flock is depending on you. Guard the flock, shepherd. Guard them until the day the Chief Shepherd returns.

CHAPTER 26: GUARDING THE FLOCK IN THE LAST DAYS

TRUMPET CALL

- Shepherd, rise and guard the flock. Wolves are circling.
- Do not stay silent while deception spreads. Blow the trumpet and warn.
- Guard them with the word, the Spirit, prayer, and the blood of Christ.
- Be courageous. Better to be hated for guarding than loved while wolves devour.

REFLECTION QUESTIONS

1. Have I faithfully warned my flock about deception and sin?
2. Do I avoid naming wolves out of fear of offending people?
3. Am I equipping my sheep to discern truth from lies?
4. Have I tolerated sin in the camp instead of confronting it?
5. Do I guard with the weapons of the Spirit, or with the tools of the world?

DECLARATION

I will guard the flock of God.

I will not stay silent while wolves devour.

I will preach the truth, warn of deception, and confront sin.

I will wield the sword of the word, pray in the Spirit, and plead the blood.

I will guard with courage, no matter the cost, until the Chief Shepherd returns.

CHAPTER 27: **Leading the Sheep Back to the Altar**

JOEL 2:17 (KJV)

"Let the priests, the ministers of the LORD, weep between the porch and the altar, and let them say, Spare thy people, O LORD, and give not thine heritage to reproach, that the heathen should rule over them: wherefore should they say among the people, Where is their God?"

The Altar is Not a Stage

In too many churches, the altar has been replaced with a platform. The pulpit has become a stage for performance instead of a sacred place of sacrifice. The spotlight has replaced the flame. The applause of men has replaced the tears of repentance.

But the Bible never calls the shepherd to entertain; it calls him to lead people to the altar of God. And the altar is not safe. The altar is where things die. It is where flesh is consumed. It is where pride is crushed. It is where fire falls.

Shepherd, if you treat the altar as optional, your people will treat holiness as optional. If you trade the fire for fog machines, the tears for theatrics, the cross for charisma, you have betrayed your call.

CHAPTER 27: LEADING THE SHEEP BACK TO THE ALTAR

Elijah Repaired the Altar

When Israel was backslidden and worshiping Baal, Elijah did not host a concert. He did not craft a motivational speech. He did one thing: "And he repaired the altar of the LORD that was broken down" (1 Kgs 18:30).

The fire did not fall until the altar was restored. The nation did not turn back to God until the prophet wept and prayed at the altar. Revival never bypasses the altar. It begins there and it ends there.

Shepherd, your first duty is not to build programs; it is to repair the altar. Call your people to repentance. Call them to surrender. Call them to weep between the porch and the altar.

The Call to Sacrifice

Romans 12:1 declares: "Present your bodies a living sacrifice, holy, acceptable unto God, which is your reasonable service." The altar is the place where living sacrifices are offered.

But in too many churches, the altar is empty. The sheep sing but do not sacrifice. They clap but do not consecrate. They attend but do not repent. Why? Because the shepherds no longer call them to the altar.

Shepherd, you must lead them back. Not by gimmicks. Not by begging. But by preaching the truth with fire. Tell them the altar is where freedom is found. Where addictions are broken. Where marriages are restored. Where holiness is birthed.

Tears at the Altar

Joel 2:17 commands the priests to weep between the porch and the altar. Shepherd, if you do not weep, your people will not weep. If you are not broken, your flock will not break.

The altar is watered with tears before it is filled with fire. True revival comes when ministers cry out: "Spare thy people, O LORD!" Not when they chase relevance, but when they chase God.

Shepherd, the sheep need to see you weep. They need to see you cry out for their souls. They need to know that the altar is not a decoration, but a destination.

The Fire Will Fall Again

When Elijah prayed at the repaired altar, fire fell from heaven and consumed the sacrifice. The people cried out: "The LORD, he is the God; the LORD, he is the God" (1 Kgs 18:39).

Shepherd, if you will lead your people back to the altar, the fire will fall again. Not strange fire of hype and emotion, but holy fire of repentance, cleansing, and power.

God is still ready to send fire, but He is waiting on shepherds to repair the altar. If you build it, He will burn it. If you lead the sheep there, He will meet them there.

CHAPTER 27: LEADING THE SHEEP BACK TO THE ALTAR

TRUMPET CALL

- Shepherd, repair the altar that has been broken down.
- Stop treating the pulpit as a stage; call your people to sacrifice.
- Weep between the porch and the altar until fire falls again.
- The sheep will follow where you lead; lead them back to the altar of God.

REFLECTION QUESTIONS

1. Have I turned the pulpit into a stage instead of an altar?
2. Do I call my people to repentance, or only to comfort?
3. Have I wept at the altar for my flock, or have I settled for performance?
4. Am I leading the sheep to sacrifice, or to self-indulgence?
5. Do I believe that God's fire will still fall if the altar is repaired?

DECLARATION

I will lead the sheep back to the altar of God.

I will not treat the pulpit as a stage, nor the altar as optional.

I will call the people to repentance, to sacrifice, to holiness.

I will weep between the porch and the altar until the fire falls again.

I will repair the altar, trusting that the God who answered by fire then will answer by fire now.

CHAPTER 28: Feeding the Sheep, Not Entertaining the Goats

JOHN 21:17 (KJV)

"He saith unto him the third time, Simon, son of Jonas, lovest thou me? Peter was grieved because he said unto him the third time, Lovest thou me? And he said unto him, Lord, thou knowest all things; thou knowest that I love thee. Jesus saith unto him, Feed my sheep."

The True Test of Love

Jesus did not ask Peter if he could build a crowd. He did not ask him if he could impress Rome, organize programs, or inspire applause. He asked him one question: "Do you love Me?" And when Peter said yes, the command was clear: "Feed my sheep."

Love for Christ is proven in care for His flock. And the primary command is not "entertain the goats" but "feed the sheep." The shepherd's call is not to keep the carnal comfortable, but to keep the hungry fed with the word of God.

The Curse of Entertainment

The modern church has mistaken applause for anointing. Lights, shows, gimmicks—all designed to draw goats while starving sheep.

CHAPTER 28: FEEDING THE SHEEP, NOT ENTERTAINING THE GOATS

But entertainment never produces disciples. It produces consumers. And consumers will turn on you the moment the show loses its shine.

Shepherd, if your ministry is built on hype, you will exhaust yourself trying to outdo the last performance. But if your ministry is built on feeding sheep, you can rest in the sufficiency of the word.

Jesus didn't say, "Put on a show for my sheep." He said, "Feed them."

The Food of the Sheep

Sheep do not live on jokes, motivational quotes, or empty affirmations. They live on the word of God. "Man shall not live by bread alone, but by every word that proceedeth out of the mouth of God" (Matt 4:4).

Preach the word, shepherd. Not your opinions. Not political rants. Not worldly wisdom. Feed them with the pure milk and the strong meat of Scripture. Teach them holiness, repentance, the cross, the blood, the Spirit, and eternity.

Anything less is starvation.

Goats Will Always Complain

When you preach truth, goats will complain. They will say you are too harsh, too old-fashioned, too judgmental. They will demand lighter sermons, shorter services, softer words.

But Jesus said: "My sheep hear my voice, and I know them, and they follow me" (John 10:27). Sheep crave the Shepherd's voice. They hunger for the word. They will follow where the truth leads.

Shepherd, stop catering to goats. If you build your ministry around them, you will betray the sheep.

The Consequence of Neglect

In Ezek 34, God rebukes the shepherds who fed themselves and not the flock. He promised to remove them and raise up true shepherds who would feed His sheep.

Neglect is dangerous. If you fail to feed the sheep, God Himself will intervene. If you fatten yourself while starving the flock, He will replace you.

Shepherd, do not play with this holy charge. You will give an account. Better to be hated by goats and faithful to Christ than loved by men and judged by God.

A Call Back to the Table

Psalm 23 says, "Thou preparest a table before me in the presence of mine enemies." The sheep need a table, not a stage. They need bread from heaven, not crumbs of hype. They need shepherds who will break the word like bread and pour out the Spirit like living water.

Shepherd, love Christ enough to feed His sheep. That is the call. That is the test. That is the measure of your ministry.

CHAPTER 28: FEEDING THE SHEEP, NOT ENTERTAINING THE GOATS

TRUMPET CALL

- Shepherd, stop entertaining goats; start feeding sheep.
- Preach the word with boldness, even if goats complain.
- Sheep are starving. Give them the bread of life, not the crumbs of hype.
- The measure of your love for Christ is not your crowd size, but your faithfulness to feed His flock.

REFLECTION QUESTIONS

1. Am I feeding the sheep or entertaining the goats?
2. Do I preach the word faithfully, or dilute it to keep people comfortable?
3. Have I mistaken applause for anointing?
4. What am I truly serving? Bread from heaven or junk food of the world?
5. Would Christ say of me, "He loves Me, for he feeds My sheep"?

DECLARATION

I will feed the sheep entrusted to me.

I will not waste time entertaining goats.

I will preach the word with boldness, without apology.

I will set the table with bread from heaven and living water.

I will prove my love for Christ not with words, but with faithfulness to feed His flock until He comes.

CHAPTER 29: The Chief Shepherd Is Coming

1 Peter 5:4 (KJV)

"And when the chief Shepherd shall appear, ye shall receive a crown of glory that fadeth not away."

The Day of Reckoning

Every shepherd must remember this sobering truth: the flock is not yours. They are His. You were not crucified for them. He was. You did not purchase them with your blood. He did. And one day, the Chief Shepherd will appear and call you to account for how you cared for what belonged to Him.

Paul declared, "For we must all appear before the judgment seat of Christ; that every one may receive the things done in his body, according to that he hath done, whether it be good or bad" (2 Cor 5:10). This is not optional. This is not metaphor. It is reality.

Shepherd, the day is coming when your sermons will be weighed, not by clicks or comments, but by Christ. Your motives will be exposed, not by men's applause, but by His eyes of fire. Your ministry will be tested, not by statistics, but by the holiness of heaven.

On that day, every excuse will vanish.

CHAPTER 29: THE CHIEF SHEPHERD IS COMING

No More Excuses

Too many shepherds hide behind excuses.
- *"The people didn't want to hear truth."*
- *"If I preached repentance, the board would fire me."*
- *"The crowd was growing when I softened my sermons."*
- *"I was too tired to warn. Too busy to pray. Too pressured to stand."*

But on that day, none of these excuses will matter. The Chief Shepherd will not ask what the board wanted. He will not ask how the crowd reacted. He will not ask if you were popular or respected. He will ask if you were faithful.

Faithful to preach His word.

Faithful to guard His flock.

Faithful to warn of sin.

Faithful to weep between the porch and the altar.

Shepherd, excuses may comfort you now, but they will condemn you then.

The Weight of Accountability

Hebrews 13:17 warns, "Obey them that have the rule over you, and submit yourselves: for they watch for your souls, as they that must give account." Shepherd, you will give an account.

This should make us tremble. Every soul entrusted to you is written in God's book. Every sheep who sat under your voice, every child who heard your sermons, every backslider who came through your doors—you will give account. Did you feed them or starve them? Did you guard them or scatter them? Did you lead them to Christ or to yourself?

TO THE SHEPHERDS

Ezekiel 34 thunders against unfaithful shepherds: "Woe be to the shepherds of Israel that do feed themselves! should not the shepherds feed the flocks?" (v. 2). God promised to remove false shepherds and feed His sheep Himself.

Make no mistake: God sees. God hears. God knows. The Chief Shepherd is coming.

The Crown for the Faithful

But hear the hope: for those who are faithful, there is a reward. "And when the chief Shepherd shall appear, ye shall receive a crown of glory that fadeth not away" (1 Pet 5:4).

This crown is not given for popularity, but for perseverance. Not for crowds, but for cross-bearing. Not for applause, but for endurance. It is for those who fought the good fight, finished their course, and kept the faith.

Paul declared at the end of his life: "I have fought a good fight, I have finished my course, I have kept the faith: Henceforth there is laid up for me a crown of righteousness" (2 Tim 4:7-8).

Shepherd, imagine that moment—kneeling before Christ, scarred from battles, weary from the fight, but hearing Him say, "Well done, thou good and faithful servant." No earthly honor can compare.

The Terror of the Unfaithful

But for those who betray their call, the day will not be glory. It will be terror. Jesus warned of shepherds who were hirelings—those who run when the wolves come, leaving the sheep to scatter (John 10:12-13). He warned of wicked servants who said in their hearts, "My lord delayeth his coming," and began to beat the other servants and live in drunkenness (Luke 12:45-46).

CHAPTER 29: THE CHIEF SHEPHERD IS COMING

What happened to them? The Master returned in an hour they did not expect and appointed them their portion with the unbelievers.

Shepherd, you cannot hide behind your title. If you have used your pulpit for profit, if you have silenced truth for applause, if you have abandoned holiness for hype, then the Chief Shepherd's coming will not be your crown; it will be your curse.

His Eyes of Fire

Revelation 1:14–15 describes Jesus: "His head and his hairs were white like wool, as white as snow; and his eyes were as a flame of fire; and his feet like unto fine brass, as if they burned in a furnace; and his voice as the sound of many waters."

Shepherd, those eyes see through your mask. They pierce your motives. They burn away your excuses. You may fool men. You may deceive denominations. You may hide behind charisma and numbers. But the eyes of the Chief Shepherd cannot be fooled.

He walks among the lampstands—the churches (Rev 1:20). He holds the stars—the pastors—in His hand. He says to some, "I know thy works . . . but I have somewhat against thee" (Rev 2:2–4). When He comes, He comes with reward and with rebuke.

The Call to Urgency

Romans 13:11 declares: "It is high time to awake out of sleep: for now is our salvation nearer than when we believed." Shepherd, the hour is late. The night is far spent. The day is at hand.

This is no time for casual preaching. No time for soft sermons. No time for compromise. The Chief Shepherd is coming. The trumpet will sound. The crown will be given. The judgment will fall.

Wake up. Watch. Warn. Work while it is day, for the night comes when no man can work (John 9:4).

Comfort for the Faithful

Yet even as this chapter thunders with warning, it resounds with comfort. Faithful shepherd, if you have wept in secret, if you have been mocked for preaching truth, if you have lost people for refusing compromise—your labor is not in vain.

Hebrews 6:10 says: "For God is not unrighteous to forget your work and labour of love, which ye have shewed toward his name, in that ye have ministered to the saints, and do minister."

Every unseen prayer, every sleepless night, every sermon preached in faithfulness though no one applauded is written in heaven. And on that day, the Chief Shepherd Himself will reward you.

TRUMPET CALL

- Shepherd, the Chief Shepherd is coming.
- Excuses will not stand. Only faithfulness will matter.
- Feed the sheep. Guard the flock. Preach the word.
- His eyes are on you now. His reward is with Him. Be found faithful when He appears.

REFLECTION QUESTIONS

1. Am I living and leading with eternity in view, or only the present?
2. Do I measure success by God's standard or man's applause?
3. Have I excused compromise that I must repent of before it is too late?
4. Would I be ready to stand before Christ today and give account with joy?
5. Am I pressing on for the crown of glory, or wasting my call on fading rewards?

DECLARATION

I will shepherd as one who must give account.

I will not excuse compromise or neglect.

I will live with eternity in view, preaching and leading as though Christ may return today.

I will fix my eyes on the Chief Shepherd, not the applause of men.

I will endure to the end, knowing a crown of glory awaits when He appears.

CHAPTER 30: A Call to the Watchmen

EZEKIEL 33:7 (KJV)

"So thou, O son of man, I have set thee a watchman unto the house of Israel; therefore thou shalt hear the word at my mouth, and warn them from me."

The Trumpet in Your Hands

Shepherd, the trumpet is not in the hands of politicians. It is not in the hands of celebrities. It is not in the hands of the world. It is in your hands. You are the watchman. You are the voice on the wall.

The question is not whether the wall is broken; it is. The question is not whether the enemy is near; he is. The question is not whether the sheep are vulnerable; they are. The question is this: Will you blow the trumpet?

The Cost of Silence

God told Ezekiel that if the watchman saw the sword coming and did not blow the trumpet, the people would perish in their sin, but their blood would be required at the watchman's hand (Ezek 33:6).

Silence is not neutrality. It is betrayal. To see the danger and say nothing is to share in the destruction. To know the truth and withhold it is to partner with the lie.

Shepherd, your silence will not protect you. It will condemn you.

The Courage to Warn

But if the watchman blows the trumpet, even if the people ignore it, he has delivered his soul. Shepherd, you are not responsible for how they respond. You are responsible for whether you warned.

Cry aloud. Spare not. Lift up your voice like a trumpet. Warn the sheep of sin. Warn them of deception. Warn them of wolves. Warn them of judgment. Warn them that the Chief Shepherd is coming.

Better to be hated for warning than judged for silence.

The Rise of the Remnant Watchmen

Not all will answer this call. Many pulpits will stay silent. Many shepherds will remain hirelings. Many watchmen will abandon the wall.

But there is a remnant. God is raising watchmen who will not bow, who will not break, who will not be bought. They may not be popular. They may not be celebrated. They may not be known. But they will be faithful.

And when they blow the trumpet, the sound will echo through the land.

This Is the Hour

Shepherd, this is the final hour. This is the time for courage, not compromise. For boldness, not fear. For fire, not fog.

TO THE SHEPHERDS

The wall is broken. The sheep are scattered. The wolves are circling. But God has set you as a watchman. You are the voice. You are the trumpet. You are the one standing between destruction and deliverance.

Do not shrink back now. Blow the trumpet until your last breath.

TRUMPET CALL

- Watchman, the trumpet is in your hands. Blow it.
- Do not fear their faces. Do not soften your sound.
- Warn the wicked. Strengthen the weary. Guard the sheep.
- The Chief Shepherd is coming. Let the trumpet sound until He appears.

REFLECTION QUESTIONS

1. Am I faithful to sound the trumpet, or have I been silent?
2. Do I fear man more than I fear God?
3. Have I warned the sheep of sin, deception, and judgment?
4. Am I standing on the wall, or have I left my post?
5. Will I be counted among the remnant watchmen when Christ returns?

DECLARATION

I am a watchman on the wall.

I will not be silent while danger approaches.

I will blow the trumpet with clarity, with courage, with conviction.

I will warn the wicked, feed the sheep, and guard the flock.

I will endure to the end, standing my post, until the Chief Shepherd comes.

A Call to Repentance

Shepherd, if you have read these pages and feel the sting of conviction, do not run from it. That pain in your soul is mercy. The Spirit of God is calling you to repentance.

The same God who rebukes is the God who restores. The same Jesus who warned Peter that he would deny Him is the Jesus who restored him by the sea. He has not cast you off. He has not closed the door. He is still calling.

The question is not whether you have failed. We all have. The question is whether you will repent. Will you return to the altar? Will you confess your compromise? Will you fall on your face and cry out for mercy?

It is not too late. Today is the day of salvation. Today is the day to return.

The time for delay is over. If compromise has dulled your message, if weariness has silenced your trumpet, if fear has chained your voice, return to the altar now.

God does not call you to hide in shame but to rise in repentance. He has not rejected you. He has not discarded you. His mercy is still greater than your failure.

Today is the day to bow low. Today is the day to rend your heart, not your garments. Today is the day to return to the God who still loves you and still calls you.

Do not let pride keep you back. Do not let fear of man bind you. Run to Him. His arms are open. His fire still falls on the altar of repentance.

CHAPTER 30: A CALL TO THE WATCHMEN

A Private Prayer of Return

Father, I come before You humbled and broken. I confess my silence, my compromise, my weariness, and my sin. I lay down my excuses. I repent for where I have failed Your flock and betrayed Your call. Wash me in the blood of Jesus. Cleanse me from all unrighteousness. Restore to me the joy of salvation, and renew a right spirit within me. Fill me again with holy fire. Give me courage to speak, boldness to warn, and faithfulness to endure. I give You my life, my ministry, and my future. Use me as a watchman until the Chief Shepherd returns. In Jesus' name, Amen.

Final Word

This book was not written for applause. It was written in trembling obedience. I am a man deeply aware of my own flaws, yet overwhelmed by the mercy of Christ, who still chose to use me.

If anything in these pages has convicted you, let it drive you to the cross. If anything has encouraged you, give glory to God. My prayer is that these words would echo like a trumpet blast in the hearts of shepherds around the world, not to exalt me, but to awaken the church.

The hour is late. The wall is broken. The trumpet must sound. Watchmen, take your place. Shepherds, return to the altar. The Chief Shepherd is coming.

About the Author

Mitch Howell is a Spirit-led writer whose passion is to awaken the church and call believers back to holiness and repentance. His works, including *Now Is the Time: The Urgent Call to Repent and Follow Jesus*, carry a message of conviction, love, and urgency for the body of Christ to return to its first love before the Lord's coming.

Ezekiel 33:7 (KJV)

"So thou, O son of man, I have set thee a watchman unto the house of Israel; therefore thou shalt hear the word at my mouth, and warn them from me."

www.ingramcontent.com/pod-product-compliance
Lightning Source LLC
Chambersburg PA
CBHW050821160426
43192CB00010B/1843